On 16 October, 1944, the 3rd White Russian Front launched its massive offensive against *Heeresgruppe Mitte*. The German *4. Armee*, whose line of defense stretched from Nowograd on the Narew to Memel, was quickly broken through.

This is the very personal war diary of the adjutant of *Volkssturm Einsatz Bataillon Goldap* (25/235), which was activated, with a strength of 400 men, on 17 October 1944. Inadequately armed with Russian infantry rifles lacking slings, light machine guns and *Panzerfäuste*, with no uniforms, entrenching tools, identity discs, blankets or medical packets, the battalion was hastily thrown into action three days later, on October 20, in the Goldap sector of the *4. Armee* front, losing 76 killed and wounded in its first action.

Withdrawn on 23 October for urgently needed training and better armament, the battalion went back into action on 18 January in the Eichwald northeast of Insterburg, near Stobingen, and fought on, with hardly a break, falling back to the city of Königsberg and taking a valiant part in the bitter defense that enabled the escape of refugees and most of the surviving military units by sea. The 70 survivors of the battalion owed their personal survival to an order forged by their last battalion commander that led to their relief by a *Wehrmacht* division and enshipment for Denmark. The author chronicles daily life dominated by desperate military action, interspersed with brief glimpses of his family, as he crosses paths with his wife and daughter, caught up in the mass of refugees fleeing before the advancing Russians.

There are very few personal accounts of Hitler's last levy, the *Volkssturm*. For years, the handwritten diary and a copy typed by the author remained in the files of the Bundesarchiv (L) in Bayreuth. The author's granddaughter approved publication for distribution, in photocopied form, to survivors and family members of the battalion. Such copies, in German, are hard to find. Now at last, this precious document from the closing days of World War II in East Prussia has become available in English translation, with careful footnotes filling in details regarding the *Volkssturm*, a unique force called into being by the Nazi Party in the closing months of the war, conceived as a party-led alternative to the Wehrmacht. Ill-equipped, pitifully armed (when armed at all) and poorly led, nevertheless on the Eastern Front – where the youngsters and older men comprising its battalions were highly motivated in a desperate attempt to delay the onrushing Russian hordes so that their wives and children could escape rape, torture, mutilation and murder at Russian hands – the *Volkssturm* sometimes achieved their goal.

Hitler's Last Levy in East Prussia

Volkssturm Einsatz Bataillon Goldap (25/235) 1944-45

Bruno Just

German edition edited by Wolfgang Rothe & Horst Rehagen
Translated, edited and revised by Frederick P. Steinhardt, MS, PhD

Helion & Company

As the chronicler of this war diary emphasized at the conclusion of his writing, this publication is dedicated to the men of *Volkssturm Bataillon Goldap* and the other East Prussian *Volkssturm* units.

Helion & Company Limited
26 Willow Road
Solihull
West Midlands
B91 1UE
England
Tel. 0121 705 3393
Fax 0121 711 4075
Email: info@helion.co.uk
Website: www.helion.co.uk
Twitter: @helionbooks
Visit our blog http://blog.helion.co.uk

Published by Helion & Company 2015

Designed and typeset by Bookcraft Ltd, Stroud, Gloucestershire
Cover designed by Paul Hewitt, Battlefield Design (www.battlefield-design.co.uk)
Printed by Lightning Source Limited, Milton Keynes, Buckinghamshire

This English edition © Helion & Company 2015. Translated, edited and revised by Frederick P. Steinhardt, MS, PhD.
Originally published as *Kriegstagebuch Volkssturm Einsatz Bataillon Goldap (25/235)*
German edition © Rothe – Rehagen – Tebben 2005. All rights reserved.
Maps open source, from Earl F. Ziemke, *Stalingrad to Berlin: The German Defeat in the East* (Washington DC: US Army Center of Military History, 1968).

ISBN 978-1-909982-72-7

British Library Cataloguing-in-Publication Data
A catalogue record for this book is available from the British Library

For details of other military history titles published by Helion & Company Limited contact the above address, or visit our website: http://www.helion.co.uk

We always welcome receiving book proposals from prospective authors working in military history.

Contents

Foreword
by Dr. Klaus Hesselbarth

After the publisher gave me the opportunity to read the completed manuscript of this work, I felt the urgent need to offer my special thanks, and to wish the publisher of this rare source of information the best of good fortune. With that goes my hope that these unique notes will reach a wide circle of readers!

My thanks for the publication go to Dr. Wolfgang Rothe. He has, in his life, devoted indefatigable energy to researching the fate of our homeland and its people, collecting extremely interesting information such as this document. That, in so doing, *Kreis* Goldap and its localities have received special attention is advantageous, and only natural. That, however, is also true for villages like Rominten and the Rominter Heide and the forestry establishments there, as well as the Trakehner Stud Farm [Trakehner *Hauptgestüt*].

In addition to this work, he has worked for years with gratifying success in supporting and pressing for museums. That has resulted in the *Ostpreußischen Landesmuseum* in Lüneburg and in the *Deutsch-Ordens-Schloß* in Ellingen / Fr., and a lasting link has developed, for which I also express my gratitude with this forward for the past work.

This document is uniquely valuable. Through the publication of *Leutnant* Just's War Diary, that has been authorized by his heiress, we learn of the fate of *Volkssturm Bataillon* Goldap. We have had only inadequate information regarding the bizarre project of the *Volkssturm* as the last levy before final defeat. Because the *Volkssturm* was only activated shortly before the collapse of the *Wehrmacht* and the *Reich*, there is no complete information regarding the units in East Prussia, for the flight and forced exodus of millions of the civilian population of the eastern region took place at the same time as the commitment of the *Volkssturm* battalions, most of whom fell into the hands of the Red Army soldiers who had been whipped up into a frenzy for revenge, or were simply killed. The incitements of Ilja Ehrenburg still sound in the ears of the generation that experienced those times, to whom memorials are still dedicated in Germany.

However, where and from whom will gratitude and remembrance come for the men of the *Volkssturm*, whose mission resulted in unparalleled sacrifices for which they were neither armed nor equipped, let alone trained. They were not even incorporated as units of the *Wehrmacht*, but, rather, were thrown into the fire in already hopeless hotspots as *"Hilfstruppe"*, auxiliaries, as were *Volkssturm-Bataillone* Goldap and Darkehmen. The men of the *Volkssturm* knew that their utterly futile commitment would be followed by a disorganized flight of their relatives in an especially bitter winter, and that this would take place without any preparations for that flight. Such preparations would have been punished as defeatism.

The ensuing document counters the unavoidable loss of recollection that results from the dwindling of the generation that underwent these experiences, and passes on to the generations of our people that follow a lasting testament. In this regard the French President Charles de Gaulle rightly observed that one can learn the character of a people by seeing how it treats its soldiers after a war that has been lost.

The war diary therefore deserves special attention and distribution. This publication should make it possible for those who are yet to come to form their own considered judgements.

These thoughts and considerations have moved and motivated me to write this forward with conviction, and with respect for the work of a companion and friend, who, despite – or because of – the difference in our ages, shares the same outlook on life.

Dr. Klaus Hesselbarth
Sorquitten

Foreword by Wolfgang Rothe & Horst Rehagen

1. More than sixty years have passed since the Red Army crossed the German border into East Prussia on 17 October 1944, and first carried the Second World War back to its starting point on German soil from which Hitler had attacked Poland in 1939. The inhabitants of East Prussia preserved a living memory of the Russian and Polish assaults and occupations that had afflicted the old Prussian land since the first settlement of the Great Wilderness in the thirteenth century. Over the centuries there had been the attack of the united Poles and Lithuanians and the Battle of Tannenberg in 1410, the Polish *Reiterkriegen*, or "Knight's Wars" of 1519-1521, the attack of the Tartars in 1656/57, the Russian occupation in the Third Silesian War, the Seven Years War in 1756-63, the decision of the Napoleonic War of 1806 / 1807 in East Prussia and the campaign against Russia in 1812/13, and, last but not least, the First World War, that raged for an entire year 1914-1915, on German soil in East Prussia. In 1914, however, a portion of the populace did not flee, but experienced the cavalry fighting with daily changers of position by both opponents and without definite fronts. The populace naturally suffered under these conditions, but were, in general, spared. They were surprised by the embittered harsh conduct of the war by the Red Army, which had been expressly whipped up to take revenge on the civilian population, as has been repeatedly established.[1]

In his introduction that follows, Dr. Krech will explain the events of the war that led up to the stagnation of the Russian offensive of the White Russian Front in July of 1944 before the borders of the German *Reich* and to the preparation of defenses against the offensive that was expected to take place in July 1944. As a part of this preparation came the precipitate activation of the *Volkssturm-*battalions to support the weakened and decimated units of the *Wehrmacht*. They were raised as a last levy, under the control of the *Reichsverteidigungskommissar*

---

1   In this regard compare the extensive documented descriptions, in W. Rothe, *Ortsatlanten der Kirchspiele Grabowen*, 3rd edition, *Alte Kirche Goldap*, 3rd edition, 2004, and, especially, *Tollmingkehmen, Siedlungsgeschichte von Preußische Litthauen, III. Band, Ortsatlas Kirchspiel Tollminkehmen*, Chapter 7, 2005.

[*Reichs* Defense Commissar] Koch, the *Gauleiter* and *Oberpräsident* [supreme executive] of East Prussia. They consisted of the age-classes of veterans of the First World War that had, hitherto, not been eligible for military service, initially without the 15-18 year old Hitler-Youth, as Just writes. They were inadequately armed, dressed, and, generally, without up-to -date training.

Dr. Hesselbarth, president of the organization of the Comrades of the Yorck-*Jäger*-Battalions, in his forward, praises this war diary as information regarding the East Prussian *Volkssturm*, which has not been covered in any previous publication.

2. Horst Rehagen, from Schackeln in the parish of Tollmingkehmen, *Kreis* Goldap, became aware of the War Diary of *Leutnant* Just by chance, and, again, when I called it to his attention a second time, as I prepared the documentation of the history of the settlement of the parish of Gurnen, and searched through the archives of the *Bundesarchiv (LA)* in Bayreuth for relevant material,[2] including the War Diary with the notation *Ostdokumentaion 8/600*. In this local atlas of the parish of Gurnen the wartime events of 1944/1945 play an essential role, since the MLR (main line of resistance) for both sides ran through the center of the parish from October 1944 to January 1945, as *Luftwaffe* aerial photographs from that period make clear.[3] *Volkssturm*-Battalion 25/235 was, as Just writes, acti-vated in Goldap and, starting on 19 October, was engaged in hopeless defensive combat against attacks by superior forces of the Red Army that were supported by heavy artillery and aircraft. This took place as an armoured spearhead of the Russian 2nd Guards Tank Division drove its attack forward between Stallupönen and Tollmingkehmen through Trakehnen as far as Nemmersdorf, southwest of Gumbinnen and far into the territory behind the German lines. There it liqui-dated the entire civilian population, a decisive paradigm for the ruthless conduct of the war against the German civilian population in ensuing months.[4] Other

---

2   Ostdokumentation Nr. 3, Kreis Goldap, Bundesarchiv (LA), Bayreuth.

3   Internet-Bestand Herder-Institut, Marburg, Kartenabteilung [map section], Kreis Goldap. See also the reports in Schmidt, *Der Kampf um Goldap.*

4   The photograph shows the inscription on a house in Tilsit that, even today (2005), acts like a banner, and its impact arouses an idea of the effect that the employment of this horrible atrocity by the Nazi party had on the civilian population, and also of its effect on the readiness of the military and *Volkssturm* units that defended their homeland and their own families. The relativisation of the mass-shooting of the entire population of the village of Nemmersdorf by the Red Army by Professor Knopp in his ZDF [*Zweites Deutsches Fernsehen*] documentary, to the effect that the propaganda troop of Dr. Goebbels had prepared the bodies of the women so that it appeared that

East-Prussian *Wehrmacht* units, in one of which Dr. Krech served as an 18 year old soldier, served on this front. Dr. Krech wrote the introduction that follows.

Horst Rehagen served on the Russian Front since 1941, and was wounded there. He fought in 1944 between *Reichsstraße* 1 and the Trakehnen railroad station. He took part in the defense of Königsberg until April 1945 and, missing the salvation of evacuation by ship to Denmark, was captured by the Russians as a prisoner of war at Heiligenbeil, finally returning in 1949. He resolved to publish the war diary of the *Volkssturm*-battalion, in part because *Oberleutnant* Rohse, initially platoon leader of the 3rd *Kompanie* of the *Volkssturm*-battalion, had been, in 1934, the highly regarded Latin teacher at the *Kant-Schule*, high school for youths in Goldap.[5] Horst Rehagen set as his objective that all of the members of the *Volkssturm*-battalion that were still alive, and also all the descendants of its members, should be given a copy of this document. In fact, several have already reserved copies with him.

3. I have followed the trail of the chronicler, Bruno Just, and I have attempted to make contact and, in fact, located his granddaughter, *Frau* Angela Tebben, who is his only living descendant. She made photographs available and allowed me to examine the account of the flight of her mother, Ingrid Struck (born Just), the daughter of the chronicler, who died in 2003. *Frau* Tebben hailed the publication of the diary.

According to the report of the daughter of the chronicler, the mother of *Frau* Tebben, Bruno Just was born in 1900. With a degree in agriculture [*Diplomlandwirt*], after administering several estates since 1932 in Faulhöden, Drengfurt, Allenstein and, finally, in Goldap, he purchased draft and meat cattle and swine, in both public and private commission, and had them shipped to the west. This activity was "necessary for the war" [*kriegswichtig*] so that he was classified as exempt from the draft [*unabkommlich, uk*]. He lived in Goldap in the *Schuhstr.* 4, as he, himself, wrote. Starting in July of 1944 he was drafted for work on fortifications and, in mid-October, assigned to *Volkssturm- Bataillon*

---

they had been raped, was considered monstrous by the old East Prussian witnesses, because the mass-shooting of women, children, old people was unjustified, even without rape, even though the program's message was, in general, accurate.

5   Rehagen also valued Just's statement that the leader of the 3rd *Kompanie* at the time of its dissolution was no longer *Oberleutnant* Rohse, but another officer, who had been brought into the battalion when it was replenished. Rohse had, in the meantime, assumed command of another company.

Goldap because its first commander, *Hauptmann* Batt, successfully appealed to have him as his adjutant, and *Hauptmann* Klein, formerly rector of the *Volksschule* in Goldap, was the company commander.

His wife, Ida Just, born Seeger, of Lithuanian descent, from Sintautai, near Eydtkuhnen, just over the border, was born in 1909. She evacuated to Krossen with her daughter, Ingrid, who was born in 1932. During the Christmas holidays of 1944, thus before the final Russian January offensive, Just spent Christmas leave with his wife and daughter. Too late, they attempted to flee to the west via Elbing, but only got as far as Königsburg, where Bruno Just met them and was able to care for them both as best he could. Repeatedly thereafter in his diary he expressed his concern while he was in the infantry-trenches before Königsberg-Ponarth as to whether his wife and child had been able to get out of Königsberg to safety in the west. He remained uncertain to the end of the diary. Therefore he did not know that they had sought in vain in Pillau for a place on a ship, and that they were, finally, surprised by the Russians in Königsberg. The report on her flight by the daughter, Ingrid Struck, born Just, described her odyssey with her mother, Ida, as "Lithuanian", unmolested, it is true, but proceeding on foot to Gumbinnen in order to escape from there to Lithuania. However, they then went back to Goldap, there to hide in an out-of-the way farmstead in May of 1945 in Samonienen / Klarfließ near Goldap, in order to inconspicuously make it through. In Goldap the mother was able to get a pass with stamp and signature stating that she was Lithuanian and had to retrieve a daughter in Elbing before she could return to Lithuania. With that the mother and daughter made their way in June 1945, via Insterburg, Preußisch Eylau, Elbing, Marienburg and Frankfurt / Oder to Berlin, arriving there four weeks later, after traveling over 1,000 kilometers on foot. Repeatedly plundered along the way or having to abandon their last belongings in overhasty flight, they had no luggage. The last and ever-so-precious possession of the 13 year old Ingrid was a crumpled photograph of her father, Bruno Just, that was hidden in the sleeve of her coat.

In November 1945, the family was reunited in Hameln. Bruno Just died in 1963.

4. The diary remained as a manuscript, a copy of the original, signed by the chronicler, that he had copied as a typescript in 1952, presumably from his hand-written notes. It is now in the archives of the *Bundesarchiv (LA)* in Bayreuth, which has given permission for this publication. It is barely legible. In several non-critical places the text had to be supplemented by "conferring". (Compare the

first and last pages of the diary that are presented in facsimile at the end of the text). The text was copied without changes, only a few grammatical irregularities carefully corrected, with a few explanations of the publisher for better comprehension [in brackets, including supplementing the Germanized village names in *Kreis* Goldap with the Prussian/Lithuanian designations current in 1938 upon their first appearance in the diary].

5. Horst Rehagen and I have taken up this diary to counter the unspeakably blanket condemnation of the *Wehrmacht* and its soldiers. I, personally (born in 1934), have never worn a uniform, neither before the war nor after. However, I am disturbed deeply by the cheap verdict of the spirit of the times, constantly indoctrinated by print, radio and television, that presents the *Wehrmacht* as a criminal organization. Our *Bundesverfassungsgericht* [Federal Constitutional Court]] is the source of the quotation, "Soldiers are murderers", with a sophisticated reference to von Ossietzki,[6] with the predictable result that soldiers of the *Bundeswehr* were grossly abused as murderers-without reference to von Ossietzki, and still are today. The discussion regarding memorials for the soldiers who were shot in 1945 as deserters will never end, nor the condemnation of all soldiers as equally guilty in the results of the war because they did not desert.

The men of the *Volkssturm* fought without hope of success, miserably equipped and supplied, hopelessly inferior, as is repeatedly described in this report, their only goal being to hold open a route of escape for their own families over the Baltic Sea and/or over the ice of the Haff. Most of them did not run away, nor did they cross over to the Russians, although they were constantly urged to do so by loudspeaker or leaflets. Every day they saw certain death facing them. Most were killed. Most of them remained steadfast until they fell or faced and went to the yet worse fate (as we well know today, in retrospect) of Russian captivity. The 1st *Kompanie* of the Goldap *Volkssturm* was lost completely at Ponath, south of Königsberg and at Keukuhren. All of the train elements were lost at Neukuhren in Samland. One company was incorporated into a *Wehrmacht* division.

---

6   Translator's note – Carl von Ossietzky (3 October 1889-4 May 1938) was a German pacifist. He received the 1935 Nobel Peace Prize for his work in exposing clandestine German re-armament. He was convicted of High Treason and Espionage in 1931 for publishing details of German re-armament, violating the Treaty of Versailles.

7. All of 70 men of the original 400 man strong battalion were released on 3 May in Flensburg, and they, too, would inevitably have been lost in Königsberg, if the last commander of the battalion had not himself written orders withdrawing himself and the remnants of his battalion from the front. 70 out of 400, and the 400 had been repeatedly replenished. In the first days of their commitment alone, between 20 and 22 October 1944, between Kiauten and Dakehnen, the battalion lost almost 100 men – the total loss amounted to about 90%. According to Bruno Just, only 1,200 men survived from the approximately 13,000 men of the East Prussian *Volkssturm*, or less than 10%!

Even today one is still shocked by the horror aroused by these numbers and from the report.

Wolfang Rothe & Horst Rehagen
Essen & Wuppertal, April 2005

Translator's Note

When I first started translating German military history I was blessed with an editor/mentor who taught me to write for military professionals, telling me that, unless I used the right words in the right style, a professional military man would not even bother to read what I wrote. That was several dozen books ago.

This is a very different project. As I started work I was troubled by the fact that it just "didn't seem to work", it refused to go into the "professional military format". Then I realized that it could not and should not do so. This is a diary, that was written by a man with an agricultural degree (*Diplomlandwirt*) whose last activity before being drafted had been buying and shipping livestock. He was not a military professional and, as a member of the *Volkssturm,* he never received significant military training. This is a very personal account of the *Volkssturm*, Hitler's "last levy", civilians who, like the author, were in exempt occupations or who were too old or too young for the *Wehrmacht*. It is written by a civilian, a very capable man, who went from cattle buyer to battalion adjutant, and, apparently, was a very competent battalion adjutant. He sees the smoking ashes of his own home after Goldap was briefly recaptured from the Russians, he has treasured moments with his wife and daughter at various times as the line of battle shifts back over his beloved homeland of East Prussia. So, if, as you read this, it seems to have been written by an amateur, it was. And I have done my best to preserve the freshness of his writing and his outlook.

Because the *Volkssturm* was so different from the more familiar *Wehrmacht* and *Waffen-SS*, it is necessary to include a brief description before moving into the body of the text.

An aspect that will seem a bit strange to one familiar with German ranks, designations and military terms results from the very nature of the *Volkssturm*. It was originally conceived, not only as a desperate last resort that would save the homeland from the Bolshevik hordes by summoning up fanaticism as only the Nazi Party could do, but also, from the personal viewpoint of the Nazi *Gauleiter*, as their own private armies. The plural is no accident. Each *Gauleiter* felt possessive of his *Volkssturm* battalions. They shared Hitler's distrust of the professional soldiers of the *Wehrmacht*. Initially they wanted the *Volkssturm* to have no connection with the *Wehrmacht*, and, as the concept evolved, did their best to keep its necessary involvement with the *Wehrmacht* to an irreducible minimum. This included nomenclature of positions and ranks. Therefore, it is neither by accident nor ignorance that familiar roles may have slightly different titles. I preserved this in the translation by retaining the German title, with an equivalent in brackets. For example, The *Gauleiter* was responsible for activating the individual *Volkssturm* battalions, each originating in a *Kreis* of his *Gau*, but the *Gauleiter* was a busy person. Therefore the *Gauleiter* were given the right to appoint an assistant to help them, and he was called a *Gaustabsführer*, or, as the author abbreviates it, a *Stabsführer*. In practice, Bormann carefully reviewed all such appointments. The *Kreisleiter* similarly, was assisted by a *Kreisstabsführer*.

In translating the usual unit history or campaign history, the *Stabschef* is usually translated as the "chief of staff". The *Volkssturm* "*Stabsführer*" might translate, quite literally, as "chief of staff", but the office is not identical, the duties differ, from the *Wehrmacht* chief of staff.

There were no colonels, majors, captains or lieutenants (*Oberst, Major, Hauptmann, Leutnant*). Instead, there were battalion leaders, company leaders, platoon leaders and squad leaders (*Bataillonsführer, Kompanieführer, Zugführer, Gruppenführer*). Where a *Volkssturm* officer held a previous rank in the *Wehrmacht*, SS, or Party, in order to avoid confusion, all such markings had to be removed or, in the case of a party official who still served in the Party and needed his rank markings while on Party duty, such markings had to be covered up.

Rank in the *Volkssturm* was indicated by silver stars embroidered on a black collar-patch. The *Gruppenführer* had a single star, the *Zugführer* two silver-colored stars, the *Kompanieführer* three stars and the *Bataillonsführer* four stars. The collar-patches and stars were homemade of makeshift materials. So, in reading this account, you will find these and other instances that make it clear that this is an account of the *Volkssturm*, not of the regular army, the *Wehrmacht*. It was written by a citizen called to defend his country, a man who was never given even the training of an ordinary draftee. His language remains that of the man he was, and the *Volkssturm* that he describes, was emphatically *not* the *Wehrmacht*.

The *Volkssturm* was a creation of the *NSDAP* (*Nationalsozialistische Deutsche Arbeiterpartei*), the Nazi Party, evolving from a series of proposals that ended up with dual primary responsibility for the *Volkssturm*. Although the original *Führer Erlass* of 26 September, 1944, stated that the *Gauleiter* were to take over the activation and command of the German *Volkssturm* in their *Gaue,* Martin Bormann, as Leader of the Party Chancellory (*Leiter der Parteikanzlei*) and Secretary to the *Führer,* assumed overall responsibility as leader of the Party Chancellery and, thus, of the *Gauleiter*, for its political and organizational aspects, as well as its activation, organization and leadership. Heinrich Himmler, *Reichsführer -SS,* head of police and Commander of the Replacement Army was responsible for the training, armament and equipping of the German *Volkssturm.*

Until attached to a *Wehrmacht* unit for field service, the *Volkssturm* remained under the command of the Party, not the *Wehrmacht*, and the Party was responsible for its supply and maintenance. The original intent was that the *Volkssturm* battalions would never be employed outside of their home *Gaue*, but there were notable exceptions, as when, following a conference with Guderian, on 16 January, 1945, Bormann ordered twenty of the internal *Gaue* to form special *Volkssturm Bataillone z.b.V. (zur besondere Verwendung*, for special service), to be equipped with German weapons for transport to reinforce the Wartheland *Volkssturm* that was crumbling under the Soviet onslaught.

Although, as Yelton reveals in his careful study, there was great variation in actual fact between various *Kreise* in the details, the following description, which follows the original concept as detailed in Hitler's 25 September, 1944 *Erlass*, fits the *Goldap* battalion very closely, which is hardly surprising, since it was one of the earliest battalions formed and among the earliest committed to action. It was formed in border – *Kreis* Goldap on the eastern margin of East Prussia, activated on 17 October, and it went into action three days later, on 20 October, exceedingly ill equipped and totally untrained. After suffering heavy losses, 76 out of 400 men, it was withdrawn to a quiet area behind the front for a brief period of basic training, reconstitution and equipping. It then fought alongside *Wehrmacht* units, largely in frontline positions, right up until it was relieved and withdrawn on 12 April, 1945, for shipment back to Copenhagen and then the *Reich* s disbandment on 3 May, 1945, just four days before *General* Jodl signed the unconditional surrender documents for all German forces on the morning of 7 May at SHAEF headquarters in Reims.

The largest element of the German *Volkssturm* was the battalion. It was commanded by the *Bataillonsführer*, who was named by the *Gauleiter*. The *Kreisleiter* had the right to name the *Kompanieführer*. The *Bataillonsführer* selected the *Zugführer* (platoon leaders) and the *Kompanieführer* selected the *Gruppenführer* (squad leaders). Selection criteria placed fanaticism and party loyalty ahead of military experience or competence. The Goldap battalion was fortunate in that all of its officers were genuine *Wehrmacht* reserve officers who had been selected for *Volkssturm* command positions.

The smallest element, the *Gruppe*, had an average strength of ten men, the leader and nine men. The *Zug*, or platoon, consisted of three to four *Gruppen*. A *Kompanie* consisted of three to four *Zügen* and a *Bataillon* of three to four *Kompanien*, the fourth company being a heavy weapons company.

Although the original concept of the *Volkssturm* was to minimize staff and trains, a staff consisting of *"Gruppe Führer"* soon appeared out of functional necessity. The *Bataillonsführer* generally was provided with a staff consisting of an adjutant, an *Ordonnanzoffizier* (special missions staff officer), an *Arzt* (surgeon), a *Gerichtsoffizier* (military justice), a *Rechnungsführer* (accountant and pay non-commissioned officer), a *Schirrmeister* (maintenance technical-sergeant), two *Schreiber* (clerks), a *Sanitätsdienstgrad* (medic) a groom or driver, a leader of the messenger echelon and 16 messengers or communications men, eight of them on bicycles and/or motorcycles.

Trains elements consisted of horse-drawn farm wagons with civilian drivers.

For those interested in following up information presented in the translator's footnotes, I have appended my own translator's bibliography. For those reading German, Seidler remains the indispensable basic reference, with Yelton's study an equally indispensable supplement and statistical analysis detailing the range of variations in actual practice. Kissel provides a clear, orderly brief summary accompanied by an extensive series of appendices containing the essential basic documents. Those who do not read German can combine reading the English translation of Kissel and Yelton.

TRANSLATOR'S BIBLIOGRAPHY

Barran, Fritz R., *Städte-Atlas Ostpreussen,* Rautenberg Verlag, Leer 1988.

Dieckert, *Major* and *General* Grossmann, *Der Kampf um Ostpreussen*, Motorbuch Verlag, Stuttgart, 1960.

Emde, Joachim, *Die Nebelwerfer: Entwicklung und Einsatz der Werfertruppe im Zweiten Weltkrieg*, Podzun-Pallas Verlag, Dorheim, 1979.

Engelmann, Joachim, *Deutsche Raketen-Werfer*, Podzun-Pallas-Verlag, Dorheim, 1977.

Gander, Terry and Peter Chamberlain, *Weapons of the Third Reich: An Encyclopedic Survey of All Small Arms, Artillery and Special Weapons of the German Land Forces, 1939-1945*, Doubleday and Company, Inc, Garden City, New York, 1979.

Hahn, Fritz, *Waffen und Geheimwaffen des deutschen Heeres 1933-1945, Band 1, Infanteriewaffen, Pionierwaffen, Artilleriewaffen, Pulver, Spreng- und*

Kampfstoffe and *Band 2, Panzer- und Sonderfahrzeuge, Wunderwaffen. Verbrauch und Verluste* in one volume, Bernard & Graefe Verlag, Bonn, 1998.

Kissel, Hans, *Der Deutsche Volkssturm 1944/45: Eine territoriale Miliz im Rahmen der Landesverteidigung, Beiheft 16/17 der Wehrwissenschaftlichen Rundschau, Zeitschrift für Europäische Sicherheit, Herausgeben vom Argeitskreis für Wehrforschung*, Verlag E. S. Mittler & Sohn, Frankfurt/M, 1962. Available in English as: *Hitler's Last Levy. The Volkssturm 1944-45*, Helion, Solihull, 2005.

Koch, H. W., *A History of Prussia*, Dorset Press, New York, N.Y., 1978.

Lasch, General Otto, *So Fiel Königsberg*, Motorbuch Verlag, Stuttgart, 1994.

Mammach, Klaus, *Der Volkssturm, Das Letzte Aufgebot, 1944-45*, Akademie Verlag, Berlin, 1981.

Rielau, Hans, *Geschichte der Nebeltruppe*, published by the ABC- und Selbstschutzschule (of the *Bundeswehr*), 1965.

Schön, Heinz, *Tragödie Ostpreußen, 1944-1948*, Arndt Verlag, Kiel, 1999.

Schön, Heinz, *'Gustloff' Katastrophe, Bericht eines Überlebenden*, Motorbuch Verlag, Stuttgart, 1984.

Seidler, Franz W., *Deutscher Volkssturm, das letzte Aufgebot, 1944/45*, Herbig, Munich – Berlin, 1989.

Tessin, Georg, *Verbände und Truppen der deutschen Wehrmacht und Waffen-SS, 1939-1945*, Biblio Verlag, Osnabrück, 1979, 16 vols.

White, Hans Joachim and Peter Offerman, *Die Boeselagerschen Reiter, Das Kavallerie Regiment Mitte und die aus ihm hervorgegangene 3. Kavallerie-Brigade/Division*, Schild-Verlag GmbH, Munich, 1998.

Yelton, David K., *Hitler's Volkssturm: The Nazi Militia and the Fall of Germany*, University Press of Kansas, Lawrence Kansas, 2002.

Introduction
Wartime Events before the Borders of East Prussia in the Fall of 1944

Dr. Klaus Krech

In the spring of 1944 *Fernaufklärungsstaffel* [Long Range Reconnaissance Squadron] 4 (*F.*) 121 – because of its squadron-insignia also called an *Uhus* [owl] squadron, or *"Eulenstaffel"* – flew a reconnaissance mission for *Heeresgruppe Mitte*. My brother, Joachim Krech (1922-1944), who did not return, also belonged to this squadron as an observer. At that time the squadron identified large troop concentrations behind the Russian front on railroads, roads, railroad stations and airfields that already indicated an impending major summer offensive. For this offensive the Russians concentrated 185 divisions with 2.5 million men. Facing them were only 28 fought-out German divisions with 400,000 men.[1] There could be no thought of reinforcing the German front, since, in the fifth year of the war, there were no more reserves available, and an allied invasion was to be expected in the west. Prior to the offensive, the front in the central sector ran in a north-south direction along the line Witebsk-Orscha-Mogilew-Bobruisk, roughly following the Dnjepr River.

The Russians launched their great offensive on 22 June 1944, wiping out the three German remnant-armies in a few weeks. They achieved major land-gains to a depth of 450 kilometers. In August 1944, they were before the border of East Prussia. The front stabilized there on the line of the Szeszuppe border-river-Willkowischken-Kalvaria, the "East-Prussia Position" east of Suwalki-Augustowo.

Already, by 16 October 1944, the Russians had again fully replenished their offensive forces, so that they could begin the attack on East Prussia with a thrust toward Königsberg by the 3rd White Russian Front (= *Heeresgruppe*) consisting of the 11th Guards Army, the 26th and 31st Armies. Facing this offensive was *General* Hossbach's 4th *Armee*, which had not yet recovered from the major defeats of the summer of 1944. The Russians opened the offensive with a sudden,

---

1   Franz Kurowski, *Die Heeresgruppe Mitte.*

hurricane-like barrage of artillery, tank-fire and ground-attack aircraft, so that our 1st *Infanterie Division* at Willkowischken, a division with experience at the front, suffered its heaviest losses to-date in the war, and had to fall back behind the border of the *Reich.*

Further south, between the Rominter Heide and Gumbinnen, the Russian attack of the 2nd Guards Panzer Army was so powerfully supported that it broke through the German line and could not be halted until it reached the Angerapp at Nemmersdorf. That village achieved its unhappy fame due to the massacre of the surprised civilian population that was perpetrated there. In the course of this surprisingly rapid Russian advance, for the first time on German soil, the *Kreis* capital, Goldap, was lost on 22 October 1944. South of the Rominter Heide the Russian advance was stopped at Gurnen, just over the border. The 367th *Infanterie Division* came from the front near Lomscha to the assistance of the fought-out 131st *Infanterie Division* that had retreated to there.[2] The elite *"Boeselager"-Reiter* unit, the Westphalian 15th *Kavallerie Regiment,* was transferred there from the Augustowo area.[3] In skillfully conducted delaying-actions between Suwalki and Wehrkirchen (Szittkehmen) the superior enemy forces were brought to a halt at the Goldap-Treuberg *Reichsstraße* [highway]. The Westphalian riders well understood a war of movement. In the Russian army the "Yellow Danger" was spoken of with respect, for yellow was the branch-of-service colour of the German cavalry.

Nevertheless, the Red Army now stood on German soil. In this clearly hopeless situation, on 18 October 1944, Hitler called for the activation of the *Volkssturm.* All men who had previously been classified as *"uk"* (exempt) from 16 to 60 years that were fit for military service [*kriegsverwendungsfähig, kv"*] were drafted.

The Nazi Party, *NSDAP*, was responsible for the activation of the *Volkssturm* units, but was not prepared for it. Thus there were neither uniforms nor footgear, no identity disks, blankets nor first-aid supplies for the first employment of the

---

2   *Hauptmann* Willy Schweck, "Als die rote Flut kam...", *Heimatbrücke* Goldap, Nr. 10 1969 ff.

3   Translator's note – This reference to the Westphalian 15th *Kavallerie Regiment* seems unclear. According to Witte & Offermann, *Die Boeselagerschen Reiter, Das Kavallerie-Regiment Mitte und die aus ihm hervorgegangene 3. Kavallerie-Brigade/Division*, p. 277, "On 4 October 1944, the 3. *Kavallerie-Brigade* was released from attachment to the cavalry corps and was transported by rail to the Netta-sector, southwest of Augustow. During the nights from 6/7 to 7/8 *Reiter-Regiment* 31, reinforced with elements of *schwere Kavallerie-Abteilung* 3 relieved *Grenadier Regiment* 528 of the 299th *Infanterie Division* in the so-called "East Prussian Defensive Position" (here at the Augustowo Canal), here with a clear defensive mission."

Volkssturm. Its initial armament consisted of totally obsolete captured weapons. The power of command was initially reserved to the party. Only after clarification of many conflicts of responsibility and differences with the *Gauleiter* Erich Koch was the *Volkssturm* committed as front-reserve to the division commanders responsible at that time. At that point cooperation functioned between the *Wehrmacht* and *Volkssturm*.[4]

The Goldap *Volkssturm-Bataillon* 25/235[5] was activated on 17 October 1944, with a strength of 400 men. Here, too, there were, initially, no uniforms. The battalion was armed with captured Russian infantry rifles, light machine guns and *Panzerfäuste*.[6] In this needy condition, and, above all, completely untrained, on 20 October 1944, the battalion was precipitately thrown into the battle at Daken-Groß Waltersdorf. Its first employment was, accordingly, costly. 76 men were wounded or killed. Only after this baptism of fire, which had grave consequences, did the command recognize that further commitment was, for the time being, irresponsible. Accordingly, the *Volkssturm* battalion was pulled out of the front for the urgently needed training and better armament. For that purpose it was transferred via Kulsen behind the great Heydtwallder forest to Buddern, northeast of Angerburg.

In the meantime the command of the 4th *Armee* brought in reinforcements from the northern and southern sectors of the front in order to force the Russian spearheads that were between Goldap and Gumbinnen back behind the Rominte River. In order to accomplish this, in a first offensive operation, east of Gumbinnen the 5th *Panzer Division* attacked the flank of the Russian assault wedge from the north toward Groß Waltersdorf. At the same time the *Führerbegleitbrigade* attacked the Russian southern flank from Daken in order to link up with the 5th *Panzer Division* near Groß Waltersdorf. The elements of the 11th Guard Army of the Red Army were subsequently wiped out or captured. After this operation, which was successfully concluded on 26 October 1944, the MLR ran north of Goldap along *Reichsstraße* 132 to Groß Waltersdorf and then northeast from there via Sprindort, Trakehnen-Königseichen-Grünberg to Schloßberg (Pillkallen).

---

4   Dieckert / Großmann, *Kampf um Ostpreußen*, 1976.
5   Translator's note – Regarding the number 25/235: The first number, 25, refers to the *Gau*, Ostpreussen, the second number, 235, the number of the battalion.
6   Translator's note – Hand-held personal anti-tank weapons.

The objective of the subsequent second operations, which followed immediately, was the recapture of Goldap at the start of November 1944. For this the 5th *Panzer Division* went into an assembly position northwest of the Goldap See [lake]. While, during the first half of the night of 2/3 November 1944, the 5th *Panzer Division* thrust surprisingly quickly, with no artillery preparation, to the northern point of the Goldap See and cut off the Russian retreat from Goldap, the 50th *Infanterie Division* moved out in the south in the second half of the night in an attack to close the Goldap *Kessel* [pocket] at the southern point of the Goldap See. This attack, however, ran into extremely strong Russian resistance, so that our troops only reached their objective there after extremely heavy fighting. On 4/5 November 1945, Goldap was again in German hands. Thereupon the MLR at the Goldap See extended south via Buttkuhnen / Bodenhausen-Kosaken / Rappen-höh and then along *Reichsstraße* 132 to Widmannsdorf. There it curved to the southeast via Mlinicken/Buschback-Szielasken/Hallenfelde by Garbassen-Mierunsken / Merunen to cross the old *Reichs* border at the Raspuda. This sector of the front and the *Kreis* capitol Goldap held until 22 January 1945.

Two strategically important hills were held or occupied with the recapture of Goldap: the Goldaper *Berg*[hill], (272 meters) which commanded the entire region around Goldap well into the Rominter Heide, and the Schäferberg near Kummetschen. There a small troop of German "greencoats" (foresters) were freed, who, after their retreat from the Rominter Heide, defended this hill and had been encircled by Russian forces.

The Goldap *Volkssturm* did not take part in either of these offensive operations, neither at Groß Waltersdorf nor in the recapture of Goldap.

When, on 12 January 1945, the Red Army launched its great offensive for the final conquest of East Prussia, it rapidly became obvious that the region around Insterburg was especially exposed. Thereupon the army command called the Goldap *Volkssturm* from its rest area at Buddern and transported it precipitately into the acutely endangered Eichwald [oak forest] northeast of Insterburg, near Stobingen.

In the defense of the immediate homeland around Goldap, this troop, which had, in the meantime, been better armed and trained, had the advantage of familiarity with the area. Now, however, the command ignored the fact that the fighting was raging most intensely in the north. The hastily introduced unit was immediately placed at the disposal of the fighting forces.

In the ensuing heavy defensive fighting the tragedy of the Goldap *Volkssturm* followed its further course.

As the Red Army spearheads captured Elbing in the southwest in the 14 days up to 26 January 1945, and stood in the north just before Königsberg, the German forces that were north and south of Goldap were in danger of encirclement. Therefore they evacuated the positions they had held ad defended so courageously in October without a fight and fell back far to the west.

Bruno Just with wife Ida and daughter Ingrid after the war.

Bruno Just with wife Ida and daughter Ingrid c 1933.

Bruno Just in Autumn 1944 as *Bataillonsadjutant* of *Volkssturm Einsatz Bataillon* Goldap. The original of this photograph was hidden in the coat of his daughter Ingrid and thus survived a journey on foot from Goldap to Frankfurt-an-der-Oder from May to July 1945.

War Diary of *Bataillonsadjutant* Just of *Volkssturm Einsatz Bataillon* Goldap (25/235) of the Events of the War from 17 October 1944 up to the Disbanding of the *Volkssturm* on 3 May 1945 in Flensburg

Dedicated to the Memory of the Fallen Comrades

By order of the *Führer*, *Volkssturm*-battalions were activated in Goldap on 17 October 1944. Initially *Einsatz (E)-Bataillon* Goldap was activated with a strength of 400 men. Later came several labor [*Arbeits-*] battalions. The *Einsatz*-battalion was quartered in the *Panzerjäger* barracks. It was armed, and should also have been clothed. The only weapons available were Russian infantry rifles, without slings, *Panzerfäuste* and German light machine guns. Instruction courses in use of the *Panzerfaust* lasting one hour were run constantly.

The battalion was divided into four companies. The battalion commander was *Hauptmann* Batt. I was the battalion-adjutant, and Batt called me back from the *Osteinsatz*[1] *for that. Hauptmann* Regge commanded the 1st *Kompanie*, *Hauptmann* Klein the 2nd *Kompanie, Oberleutnant* Rohse the 3rd *Kompanie* and *Hauptmann* Szurowski the 4th *Kompanie*. The battalion surgeon was the *Kreis*-doctor, Dr. Räthling. 25 vehicles were assigned to the battalion. Gustav Preuss commanded the trains element. The wagon-drivers were mostly Polish.

---

1   Translator's note-In mid-July, as Russian forces drew near to the East Prussian border, *Gauleiter* Koch proposed the construction of an East Prussian protective position, a *Schützwall*. On 16 July a mass-levy of tens of thousands of East Prussian citizens were drafted from their workplaces, farms and homes to construct this position. Wolfgang Rothe and Horst Rehagen state, in their forward, that, according to the report of his daughter, the mother of *Frau* Tebben, Bruno Just had been drafted into work on East Prussian fortifications in July 1944. Presumably that is what he referred to as "the *Osteinsatz*", rather than its usual reference to the *Osteinsatz*, or "Eastern Action", program in which both Hitler Youth and the *Bund Deutscher Mädel* [League of German Girls] worked to aid and support *Volksdeutsch*, or ethnic Germans who had been re-settled from the Baltic lands, Bessarabia, Galicia and eastern Poland into what was then the *Reich*, primarily western Prussia, upper Silesia and the Wartheland, that part of Poland which Nazi Germany annexed in 1939 and turned into a *Reichsgau*, intending that it become fully a part of Germany.

The Evacuation of *Kreis* Goldap was urgent, for the Russians were at the East Prussian border and a large number of our men were sent home on leave to help in the evacuation. The battalion was then only 200 men strong.

18 OCTOBER

The 3rd *Kompanie* detached one platoon under Ernst Kutz as security in Schäferberg [Klein Kummetschen]. Their mission was to secure the Gumbinnen-Goldap road. These men were properly uniformed and had two light machine guns and *Panzerfäuste*. In addition the battalion had to post security on roads and bridges.

The 1st *Kompanie* sent a detachment to Wehrkirchen [Szittkehmen] to bring back the luggage that had been left there by refugees. The men were fired on by Russian artillery and could only partially fulfil their mission. Otherwise, short-term weapons instruction continued.

19 OCTOBER

As on the previous day. Unfortunately the available clothing in the way of under-wear and shoes was way inadequate and, for no understandable reason, even that was not issued. Blankets were available in abundance, but they, too, were not issued.

20 OCTOBER

During the night of 19/20 October and in the morning of 20 October the city of Goldap was completely evacuated of all its inhabitants. At 0800 hours the battalion was ordered to occupy the fighting-trenches from Heidensee to the firing range. At 1200 hours came the order that the fighting trenches from Heidensee [Schilinnen] to Hohenrode [Trakischken] were to be occupied.

The battalion command post was to be the mill of the Agricultural *Kreis*-Cooperative at the railroad station. At 1700 hours an order arrived from District-Commander [*Gebietskommandeur*] Behrendt stating that the battalion was to secure the Daken [Dakehnen]-Husarenberg [Perkallen]-Groß Walterdorf [Walterkehmen] road against advancing Russian armour. At 1900 hours we were loaded on lorries to Daken. In Daken the *Wehrmacht* element there refused to allow us to drive further, because the position that we were to occupy was already

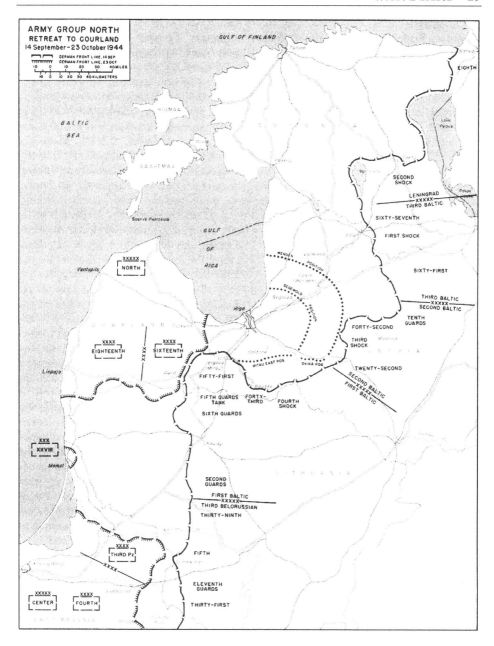

held by the Russians. Two *Tiger* tanks stood on the road to Groß Waltersdorf and blocked the road. The battalion commander reported to the local commander in Daken, an *Oberstleutnant* [lieutenant colonel] who declared that the battalion had to immediately be attached to the *Wehrmacht* if it was to take part in combat operations. The battalion commander reported to Goldap and, himself, drove to confer with the division commander. The battalion took position in Daken. The battalion command post was in the first farmstead at the south entrance to Daken.

21 OCTOBER

The battalion occupied the first line fighting-trenches at Schwadenfeld [Didzullen]. The battalion command post was the first farmstead on the road south of Schwadenfeld-Zellmühle [Kiauten]. Unfortunately the men had to go into the trenches in their civilian clothes and with no blankets, everything was left behind in Daken. This was a horrifying situation, since it could be expected that the Russians would treat any men that they captured as bandits. The Party was greatly at fault in this. A further serious problem was that the Russian rifles had not been sighted in and, for the most part, failed to function. Many of the men even went into the trenches in their low shoes (Oxfords). I, myself, made sure that I was properly clothed before departing for the field.

To our left the *Wehrmacht* was in the trenches. They were men that had been swept up behind the front and thrown into the trenches. Every possible formation was there. Such a force was not under its leader's control. To the right was an Angerapp *Volkssturm* battalion. At about 1200 hours Company-Commander Regge reported that his company was under fire from Russian infantry on the left. An hour later he reported that his company was being fired upon from the left rear and was also under fire from Russian armour. The *Wehrmacht* on the left were already coming into his sector. The Battalion Commander informed himself of the situation and, in order to avoid encirclement, he ordered that the 1st *Kompanie* was to fall back through the communications trenches to the second line of trenches. The 2nd, 3rd and 4th *Kompanien* were likewise to fall back to the second line of trenches. The Battalion Commander, himself, remained with me in the first line trenches and observed for a long time. Then an automobile drove up with a *Luftwaffe Oberleutnant*, which immediately drew fire. He remained near us and the battalion commander discussed the situation with him. The *Luftwaffe Oberleutnant* also advised him to pull the battalion back to the second line trenches.

We continued to observe. Only when the incoming rounds impacted near us did we go back to the second line trenches. We found nobody there. The battalion commander was extremely upset and angry that the 1st *Kompanie* was not there in the second line trenches. We went further back to Zellmühle and found the

2nd, 3rd and 4th *Kompanien* there, all of which had gone back to Zellmühle. These companies had simply been drawn along by the retreating *Wehrmacht* elements. Artillery, infantry and trains elements all marched in a great mixed-up mass, with armour in its midst, to Zellmühle. The battalion commander repeatedly inquired along the way for the 1st *Kompanie*. Nobody had seen it. Finally, in Zellmühle, we ran into the 2nd, 3rd and 4th *Kompanien*. There was still nothing to be seen of the 1st *Kompanie*. *Hauptmann* Szurowske was assigned command of these three companies, and the Battalion Commander went on with me to the Zellmühle estate. There, finally, we found *Hauptmann* Regge. He said that he had already met with the division commander, and that he was waiting for *Hauptmann* Batt. What did Regge have to do with the division commander? He had acted against the express orders of the battalion commander and had bolted. That was the incontrovertible fact. The battalion commander reported to the division commander, who screamed terribly at him and had him arrested for cowardice in the face of the enemy. He was to be brought up before a court martial. I could no longer speak with him.

The battalion commander of the Angerapp *Volkssturm* battalion assumed command of our battalion and immediately sent it back to the tenches. In the meantime, the trains elements arrived in Zellmühle from Goldap and we could pass out some weapons and also rations. I remained back in Zellmühle and set up an intermediate command post. The trains elements were well housed in Zellmühle. Suddenly the Russian artillery opened fire on the village and estate of Zellmühle. The night was much disturbed. Many *Wehrmacht* vehicles drove through Zellmühle. Ostensibly they were to launch a counterattack. They were the *Großdeutschland*-and *"Hermann Göring" Divisionen*, thus elite troops. The battalion surgeon told *Hauptmann* Klein that he had to drive to Goldap to fill up with petrol, and drove there with his three vehicles and all of the medical personnel. We did not see him again for quite a while.

22 OCTOBER

In the morning I learned that *Hauptmann* Batt was staying in the manor house. He was extremely depressed and desperate. He had already been interrogated and was to be shot. He was, however, still to be turned over to the Party, which was responsible for the *Volkssturm*. I then saw and heard no more of him for a long time.[2]

That morning we had many sick people and our battalion surgeon was not there. I asked the battalion surgeon of the Angerapp battalion, Dr. Richter, from Goldap, to care for our men. He did so. At the same time I reported to the Angerapp battalion commander and he ordered me to bring *Hauptmann* Klein and *Hauptmann* Regge for a discussion. I went to the first line trenches. The entire terrain was already under fire. I had to search a long time in the trenches until I found *Hauptmann* Klein, who was at the extreme left wing. All of the trenches were under heavy fire from Russian armour and mortars. The mortars were, generally, the strength of the Russian army. At the discussion the gentlemen were unanimous in the opinion that *Hauptmann* Klein should assume command of the battalion. Late in the afternoon they went back to the trenches. I remained at the intermediate command post and with the trains elements in Zellmühle. I was to establish contact with *Regiment* 1096. That day the Russians continued to shell the village and estate of Zellmühle. We suffered no losses.

During the night the fire was so heavy that I feared that the trains elements would be hit. There was no hope of sleeping. I sent a report to the battalion commander and requested that, if the fire became heavier, I might fall back with the trains elements to Kaschen [Kaschemeken]. The battalion commander agreed.

That day Goldap was captured by the Russians.

23 OCTOBER

At 0500 hours I ordered Trains-Commander Preuss to fall back with the trains elements to Kaschen. I, myself, rode to the regiment on a bicycle along with messenger Steiner. *En route* there were incoming rounds everywhere, and we often had to take cover in the roadside ditches. That day the Russians also employed masses of their ground-attack aircraft, and bombed the entire rear area with its many artillery, anti-tank, mortar and anti-aircraft positions with one-kilo-gram bombs. Their effect was extremely great. We and the *Wehrmacht* suffered heavy losses. The heavy weapons of the *Wehrmacht* were unable, at times, to

---

2   According to the diary entry of 15 January 1945, p. 15, the new Battalion Commander Klein requested *Hauptmann* Batt, the first battalion commander, as his successor. Therefore Batt had been rehabilitated.

fire. Nevertheless, the *Flak* soldiers [*Flak*-anti-aircraft guns] remained calm and fired all that they could. They had sufficient ammunition and shot down several aircraft. Unfortunately no German fighters supported their efforts. Even a very few fighters would have quickly put an end to the Russian ground-attack planes. We were set out there, defenseless against the Russian fliers.

Our first loss in the trenches was *Hauptmann* Regge, shot through the chest by a Russian sharpshooter. Was that fate? Under the developing circumstances he could not be brought out and buried. Platoon Leader Kopkow assumed command of the orphaned 1st *Kompanie*. The first wounded were brought back to the rear. I, myself, was lightly wounded in the buttocks. As I was *en route* with Preuss to seek out a now location for the trains elements, for they could no longer remain in Kaschen, we came under a hail of aerial bombs. About 30 of these one-kilogram bombs burst with an ungodly racket only two meters from us and showered us with filth and fragments. One of these splinters wounded me in the buttocks. The Russian fliers were now that bold and strafed all that they could see and dropped their bombs on everyone, because they presumed there were concentrations of troops there. The farmsteads were ablaze in all the localities around. Men, horses and vehicles of all sorts were hit and left lying. No place was safe anymore. Several of our horses were also wounded. An unbroken series of Russian aircraft overhead gave us no chance to rest. They wanted to roll up our positions. Soldiers who had survived many battles assured us that they had never before experienced such an inferno.

Were we, really, so weak at this point that we had nothing with which to oppose the Russians? Due to a shortage of ammunition, we could not employ tanks and *Sturmgeschütze* [assault guns]. Heavy artillery was nowhere to be seen. The fighting trenches and all of the defensive positions behind the trenches were simply ploughed up by incoming rounds. Whatever was still alive in the trenches was killed by the bomb and shell fragments flying around. The men in the trenches could no longer lift their noses. There were dead and wounded in the trenches. We had not been issued first-aid packets, so nobody could be bandaged. Whoever was able to get back to the rear found his way to a dressing station and was bandaged there and taken by *Wehrmacht* vehicles to a hospital. Severely wounded could not be retrieved from the trenches. On this day of major fighting more people were wounded and killed than in weeks of quieter periods. Wherever I could help, I did my best. However, my own wound was a serious hindrance. I had only a makeshift sticking-plaster slapped on.

With great difficulty we brought the trains elements into the outbuildings of Kaschen. It took several hours to traverse a single kilometer. Again and again we had to take cover from bombs and shell fragments behind stout trees and in the roadside ditches. Hell had broken loose, and now our men were in this hell without proper clothing, weapons or the correct equipment and training. The sacrifice that our battalion had to make on its first day of combat was, accordingly, immense.

An anti-tank gun crew was dispatched to Angerapp for training. At 1600 hours the first soldiers and *Volkssturm* men came running over the fields from the trenches. They were extremely distraught. It was impossible to stop most of them. It was easy to see what they had gone through. I kept firm control of most of our men. Soldiers ran to the rear incessantly. I now sent the trains element into the Gulbensee ravine. I hoped that the vehicles would be more or less secure there. The Russians never let up, and, as before, their aircraft were aloft. I went with Preuss back to Kaschen., but "went" is saying too much. We crawled more than we went, for we constantly had to seek cover. Everything was coming apart there. The *Wehrmacht* had moved the dressing station and the village was on fire from end to end. I ran into Szurowski and we decided to proceed to Zoden [Zodschen] and assemble there. Only individual men still came back, nobody knew anything about the main body. Nobody knew who was left behind wounded or dead, or who had been captured. The battalion had only just been activated a few days earlier. The men did not know each other, the officers did not know their men. Nobody ever heard any more about any of the men that fell into Russian hands as dead, living or wounded. Their families would wait in vain for their men and sons, and no one could give them any word as to where they were. We also had a large number of youths from the *Hitlerjugend* with us.

Here, too, the party is to blame for not taking care that identity discs were issued or proper lists made. The wounded comrades begged and implored-as did those of the *Wehrmacht*-to be taken along, for they were facing a terrible fate, of being treated as bandits by the Russians and simply being killed. It was impossible to take all of the wounded with us. War is hard and cruel. It does not ask whom it has just killed and whom it leaves alive. The war also has its own laws, and it allows this one or that one to fall indiscriminately. It matters not whether he lived his life well or badly. There is no differentiation made between good and evil men, for all men that stand with weapon in hand before the enemy are good men, and it is a shame for any man that it is his lot to die. All that made it safely out of that witch's cauldron could be happy and fortunate that fate had spared them this time. Probably it would strike one or another the next time.

The trains elements came out of the battle relatively well, with only a few injured men and horses. After we had assembled, we marched to Klein Zedmar. Darkness had, in the meantime, fallen, and the fliers left us alone. But still the explosions of the bombs resounded in our ears. The clatter of the steel -tired wheels on the hard roads sounded like explosions to us. Now we saw that we were in a proper bag. Farmsteads were ablaze on three sides of us and we had only one road by which we could escape from the Russians. All of Goldap was in flames. Would we ever see our home-city again? However, the men's mood gradually improved again and most had already forgotten the great and terrifying experience by the time we arrived in Zedmar in the middle of the night. Several, on the other hand, retained a lasting terror from the action they had been in. As best we could we prepared to sleep. The day's loss amounted to 76 men.

There is still one thing I must say. In the course of the morning's fighting one of our men suddenly crept out of the trench and ran over to the Russians. He was shot by our own men.

24 OCTOBER

In the morning I drove with Preuss to the nearest dressing station and had my wound tended to. It was not bad, only a flesh wound. The fragment was deeply embedded. If it did not cause me trouble it should remain there. We then attempted to contact Battalion Commander Klein. We found him in Jungferngrund. He immediately ordered that the battalion march to Jungferngrund. In the meantime, the men had rested and cleaned themselves up in Zedmar. They had also come up with food.

25 OCTOBER

The battalion marched to Jungferngrund. More and more men showed up there. We received adequate rations from the Party. The battalion surgeon, Dr. Räthling, turned up. On the 21st he had, allegedly, been unable to return to Zellmühle because he had to transport wounded. How could he transport wounded when his place was with our battalion? Battalion Commander Klein took no action against him. The vehicles could have gone to refuel without him. Neither he nor all of his medical personnel needed to go with them.

26 OCTOBER

The battalion now had a strength of 120 men and was to go into position in Kulsen. We moved out at 1400 hours. The battalion commander drove forward with a motorcycle to find quarters. On the way, in a field-dressing station, I grabbed a German 10-round carbine. That carbine remained with me to the end. Everything in Kulsen had already been occupied by the *Wehrmacht*. Billets were miserable. I had been in Kulsen a long time when I was in service in the east digging fortifications, and knew the village and its accommodations very well.

27 OCTOBER

After discussion with the village commandant, quarters were provided for us. It struck us there that the *Wehrmacht* trains elements were quite far from the fighting troops, and that they were quartered a good day's march behind them. The troops at the front must hunger and suffer because the trains vehicles could not make it to the front due to enemy contact. The fighting troops at the front should rather have been given good rations, for they needed them more than any others. I repeatedly experienced that the *Landser* (common soldiers) at the front went hungry. The approach route of the trains elements from their resting position to the front was much too far. Many horses and men could have been spared there. It was conspicuous that many young men stayed with the trains elements. The companies were billeted well. The battalion command post was at the manor house. We were attached to Combat-Sector Weiss, the *Kreisleiter* of Angerburg. He was a personable man, as was his adjutant. Three companies were constituted, the 1st *Kompanie* under Kopkow, the 3rd under *Oberleutnant* Rohse, and the fourth under *Hauptmann* Szurowski.

28 OCTOBER

The companies had to immediately start building positions. The trenches were already done. Now winter-safe bunkers had to be built. The *Wehrmacht* had already also built at this position and supported us with both word and deed. We worked well with the responsible authorities. We received an automobile and a lorry. The lorry was driven by a *Wehrmacht* non-com. Höpfner drove the automobile.

29 OCTOBER

We busied ourselves finding equipment and weapons for our men. Weiss promised everything. The Goldap *Kreisleitung* [*Kreis* government] sat in Albrechtswiesen.

30 OCTOBER

Construction of positions continued. In addition, training was to proceed on a large scale. We were not "in retirement" here. We were to be trained for new combat. From the abandoned farmsteads we rounded up 15 beef cattle, 10 pigs, 35 sheep, 60 geese and 30 ducks. The companies supplied themselves in like fashion. The 1st *Kompanie* was shifted to Ostau. The battalion staff was also properly activated. Borowski became clerk (later Ryba), Gürtler was paymaster, Quittkat and Sember took over rations, while Klarhöfer took care of clothing and weapons. Hilpert and Sablowski cooked. They were good at it and did well for us. Each company stationed three messengers with us.

31 OCTOBER

The first uniforms arrived, as did weapons and ammunition. As weapons we received Russian rifles, German light and heavy machine guns, Dutch light and heavy machine guns, 2 cm automatic weapons, *Panzerfäuste* and *Panzerschreck*. Some of the uniforms provided were brown. We could only clothe one company in gray. Unfortunately, the other two had to wear brown. There was a general prejudice against the brown uniforms.[3] Gradually stragglers appeared. Rations were good, since we were able to do our own slaughtering. All of the farmsteads had been abandoned by their residents. We could only take from the farms what we ourselves needed for rations. Furniture and other items could not be removed from the dwellings. Nevertheless, everywhere *Landser* had already been there, rummaged through everything and taken whatever they could use, which was,

---

3 Translator's note – There was good reason for the prejudice against *Volkssturm* wearing brown uniforms. Russian soldiers frequently killed *Volkssturm* men who were captured wearing brown uniforms in bestial fashion [see *Anlage 20*, in Kissel] assuming that they were Nazi Party members, since the official Party uniforms were brown. Due to the desperate shortage of uniforms, and the official refusal to provide uniforms for the *Volkssturm*, any available uniforms were used in an effort to replace civilian dress with something more-or -less "uniform", including large stocks of brown Nazi Party uniforms, brown *SA* uniforms and brown *RAD* [*Reichsarbeitsdienst*] uniforms.

in fact, for the best, before the Russians took it all. Each company was assigned five vehicles.

5 NOVEMBER

Training, construction of positions and issuance of clothing continued. News from the front was that the Russians had not advanced from the positions they had held back when we were there in October. I took Gürtler, Höpfner and Borowski along with me and we rode bicycles to Goldap as a patrol to find out what was going on in Goldap. *En route* we saw many troops digging field fortifications. The positions were to be strongly improved as far as Goldap. Everywhere there were heavy caliber guns. Shortly before Goldap things began to look very much like war. Everywhere on and alongside the road were craters from bombs and artillery. Roadside trees lay on and beside the road. The telephone wires hung down, farmsteads were burnt out. We had to undergo an attack by ground-attack planes. As we drew near to Goldap we learned that our 5th *Panzer Division* had launched an attack on the Russians early that day and had driven them out of Goldap. The city, itself, looked awful. The small houses at the edge of the city were, for the most part, intact. Our *Landser* had already made themselves at home there. The market and all of the streets leading to it were destroyed. Everything had been systematically burned down and destroyed. Many ruined houses were still smoking. In the First World War Goldap had already suffered from the Russian invasion. Then, too, entire blocks of houses had burned down. But this was, indeed, very bad.

The evacuated residents of Goldap had left their homes in the firm belief that they would be able to return after 14 days. In the event, that did not work out. Such a destroyed city is not rebuilt so quickly. That would take years. How many hopes and memories of beautiful times and shared experiences, and well-loved homes and possessions were destroyed forever. My home, too, was burned to the ground. We were told that, daily, the Russians had driven off with many lorry loads of furniture from the houses, and had also emptied the warehouses of provisions and granaries. Shopkeepers also still had large inventories in their stores. Mills and granaries were full of grain. The portions of *Kreis* Goldap to the west, north and east were still full of grain on the farmsteads, for the harvest had just been brought in. Thus the Russians had captured immense booty in Goldap. Prisoners were also supposed to have stated that nowhere had they found so much merchandise as in Goldap.

What must the individual "Ivans" (Russian soldiers) think, that came from the depths of Siberia and now, suddenly, were in this well stocked city, a rich city, by their standards. While we were in the city there were several incoming artillery rounds in the market. There was still fighting in the Memelerstraße and at the dairy. Dead Russians and horses lay around. Many Russians were still supposed to be holding out in the cellars. Probably they were watching us. The city seemed to have died.

8 NOVEMBER

I had business in Angerburg and happened to meet my wife. We were able to spend several hours together.

10 NOVEMBER

The East Prussian *Volkssturm* were sworn in at Insterburg. The *Gauleiter*, himself, conducted the swearing in. The battalion sent 100 men, who were driven there by lorry. First the men had to all be dressed in brown. Abundant weapons had to be brought along. Schibilla led the company and proved to be unprepared, because he did not bring a weapon with him.

12 NOVEMBER

My wife visited me in Kulsen and remained for several days.

15 NOVEMBER

Bataillon Heiner, which had hitherto been a work-battalion, now became an *Einsatz-Bataillon* and moved into our sector. It was only 100 men strong, and was too small for a battalion. Eventually that was recognized and the battalion was disbanded. It was consolidated into our battalion as the 2nd *Kompanie*. We again had four companies. The new company was commanded by Stachel. We were then again up to combat strength.

20 NOVEMBER

The battalion was transferred and was to build the Benkheim-Storchenberg-Buddern position. The battalion command post was in the *Bürgermeister-Haus* [mayor's house]. The 1st *Kompanie* initially remained in Kulsen. The 2nd *Kompanie* was in Benkheim, the 3rd *Kompanie* in Gronden and the 4th *Kompanie* in Storchenberg. Construction of this position was certainly a mistake. There was no apparent purpose. In any case, we spent several weeks on it.

We, ourselves, had much to do. The paper war, especially, became ever more burdensome. Marquardt came on as a second clerk. The higher-ups demanded the most impossible reports. By way of weapons we now received Italian 4.5 cm mortars. We also got German carbines with grenade-launchers for rifle-grenades. Our armourer's-assistant, Aschmotat, was downright useless. Our arsenal was already quite large. In Benkheim we kept up constant courses to familiarize the men with the weapons. Company-level training was constantly progressing. The men displayed interest and mastered their weapons well. Hand grenades were not available. *Panzerfäuste* were fired so that the men could become accustomed to the bang. During the week all weapons were fired several times with live ammunition. Ammunition was abundantly available.

The Goldap *Kreisleitung* [government] was in our neighbourhood, but the *Kreisleiter* never found time to make even one visit to our battalion, even though he frequently drove past us. The *Stabsführer*[4] visited us more often. The men were indignant about the fact that the *Kreisleiter* took no time to visit us. It was generally uncomfortably conspicuous that none of the political leaders served in the *Volkssturm*. Probably they were too good to take up weapons against the Russians. It would, however, have substantially increased the prestige of the party if these gentlemen had been more active with us. *Kreisleiter* Wagner, the commander of the East Prussian *Volkssturm,* did visit us once. He was most pompous, as if everyone must surely know him.

---

4   Translator's note – As previously noted, the *Stabsführer* the author refers to was *not* the familiar *Stabschef* of the *Wehrmacht*, who was the right-hand man of the General commanding a division or higher formation. The *Stabsführer* was a man selected by the *Gauleiter* to assist him in activating and dealing with the *Volkssturm*. The *Gauleiter* in general, and East Prussia's *Gauleiter* Koch very specifically and outspokenly, considered that the *Volkssturm* were their own private armies with which they, personally, were going to do what the regular armed forces could not. They were empowered to select their own *Stabsführer*, very definitely a political appointee, the first qualification being fanatical loyalty to the party.

6 DECEMBER

My wife visited me for several days in Albrechtswiesen. She was always treated very kindly and courteously by Battalion Commander Klein. How the comrades looked after her! My relationship with the battalion commander was also very good. We understood each other perfectly. He wanted me to be present at all discussions. There were frequent discussions with party and *Wehrmacht* officials. Every possible high and extremely high officer came to see us.

One time when the battalion commander returned from a discussion of the combat sector he told me that the topic of discussion was the appointment of the deputy battalion commander, that it should not be the highest-ranking officer, but the most capable man in the battalion. "I proposed that you should be my deputy", he said to me. I was proud and fortunate. For me that was recognition enough for my work. Now I could also sign documents if he was not there. I was also trusted with all business, as if I had been doing nothing but service as adjutant and general staff work all my life. I was sent to discussions and knew all that was going on. The company commanders, especially Rohse and Szurowski, who were, indeed, officers, did not want to recognize me. However, in every respect I was way above them and always got my way. If I had served my time in the *Wehrmacht*, I would, by then, have been exactly where they were. Rohse was not a good soldier. The company was actually run by his administrative officer [*Verwaltungsführer*], Kutz. Szurowski put in more effort, but was, otherwise, rather limited. The driving force in his company was Krämer. The officers had to take off their shoulder straps. In the *Volkssturm* there were other badges and ranks. I had the rank of a *Kompanieführer*, company commander, and wore three stars.

10 DECEMBER

The battalion was to construct the position in Buddern and occupy it. The position was already quite well built, but there was still a lot to do. Above all, bunkers were also to be built there in the trenches for winter. The 1st, 2nd and 3rd *Kompanien* were shifted to Buddern, the 4th *Kompanie* near Doviaten. The 4th *Kompanie* was now the heavy company. It received all the heavy weapons and elements of the company were distributed throughout the entire sector. We initially remained in Buddern.

There were frequent opportunities to drive to Goldap, and we salvaged all sorts of material from the rubble there, such as stoves for the bunkers, horseshoes, nails, petrol, oil and many other things. We were abundantly supplied with all materiel. Saddle horses were assigned to the battalion for the battalion commander, the adjutant, the commander of the trains elements and for each company commander. The horses were quite good.

15 DECEMBER

The staff took up quarters at Buddern in the *Bürgermeister*-house and we were very well housed.

24 DECEMBER

Our Christmas celebration started in our officer's club. There was a generous *Schnaps* issue, so that every man received a bottle. Then there were lots of cigarettes, candies, cookies, coffee beans, games, harmonicas and the like. My wife and daughter joined in the celebration. After evening dinner came a visit to the celebration of the 3rd *Kompanie*. It was a "moist" [boozy] celebration.

25 DECEMBER

Today was free of duties. The deputy *Gauleiter* promised an official Christmas celebration. 1500 hours, celebration in the *Gasthaus* [inn]. Another 100 bottles of liquor were distributed as a personal gift from the *Gauleiter*. Then there were yet more cigarettes and books. I had arranged for a band and it was an extremely beautiful celebration. After this celebration there was a highly decorated coffee table for all in the officer's club with *Kreisleiter* Quednau. Shortly before Christmas I had met the Goldap *Kreisbauernführer*, the leader of the Goldap *Kreis* farmers, and received 500 pounds of very good wheat flour as a Christmas present from the farmers of the *Kreis* to the *Volkssturm*. Each company could now bake abundant pastries. The noonday meal was also very good for all of the companies. It was also the first free day so that the men could all get plenty of rest.

26 DECEMBER

I received a week of leave and spent it with my wife and daughter in Angerburg. They were very wonderful days. I had now been in unbroken service since 13 July, initially in service in the East and then in harness here. The rest did me good. My wife did everything possible to make the leave with me as beautiful as possible.

3 JANUARY 1945

In the meantime, the battalion had been filled out to 600 men, but then had to give up 100 men to a second Rominte battalion. Along with these replacements we also finally got the last men who had been given leave to help in the evacuation back in October. Many of them had been at loose ends until now. We also received a telephone troop and laid telephone connections to the combat sector and to the companies.

5 JANUARY

The battalion received three Russian 10.2 cm field howitzers and had to activate a battery. The battery commander was Gustav Preuss. The battery had a strength of 42 men. It received vehicles and I gave it sheep, pigs and beef cattle from our stock. The battery went into position in Doviaten, but first it had to improve the position. 120 rounds of ammunition were available. The battalion was now impeccably outfitted with modern equipment. The men were trained in all of the weapons. Nearly all of the men now had uniforms, except that it was impossible to get large sizes for fat men. Little footwear was supplied.

Dr. Räthling went on leave. His deputy was Dr. Torkler. All of the men also received six days leave, in rotation. For many, however, it was impossible to travel to Saxony, to which many of their families had been evacuated, in that number of days.

10 JANUARY

The *Wehrmacht* Welfare Services [*Wehrmachttruppenbetreuung*] instituted movie shows and other functions. I was well known to the local commandant and was always able to get our men into such shows. Our battalion was no longer called the *Goldaper Einsatzbataillon*, but, rather, received the number 25/235. 25 was the *Gau* number and 235 the serial number of the battalion. We were to use only that in writing. It was to serve as our code-address.

17 JANUARY[5]

In the morning we heard artillery from the front for hours on end. As we learned, the Russians had attacked the entire front from the Samland coast all the way to Austria with immense artillery fire. The quiet time was over for us. The *Wehrmacht*, too, had enjoyed a quiet time and had prepared itself for the decisive battle. The battalion had to give up 25 men with weapons and ammunition to the armoured echelon. Our lorry took the men there and did not return.

18 JANUARY

The battalion entrained with all weapons and equipment for transport to Insterburg. We were not to hold our Buddern position. We took our battery with us. We could only take six vehicles because the available transport was too limited. The other vehicles had to follow after by road. A small party stayed behind in Buddern. We were told that we would repulse the Russians in three weeks and then return to Buddern.

19 JANUARY

Detrain in Insterburg and march to Tannenschlucht. Battalion command post in the Eichwalde forester's house.

20 JANUARY

The battalion was attached to the Wurach combat sector and occupied the forest position in the Eichwalder forest. The position was well constructed, except that in places there was a live abatis in front of the trenches. There was no field of fire and no visibility. The trees approached right up to the trenches and, especially at

---

5   Translator's note – The Russian major offensive against East Prussia opened on 13 January 1945.

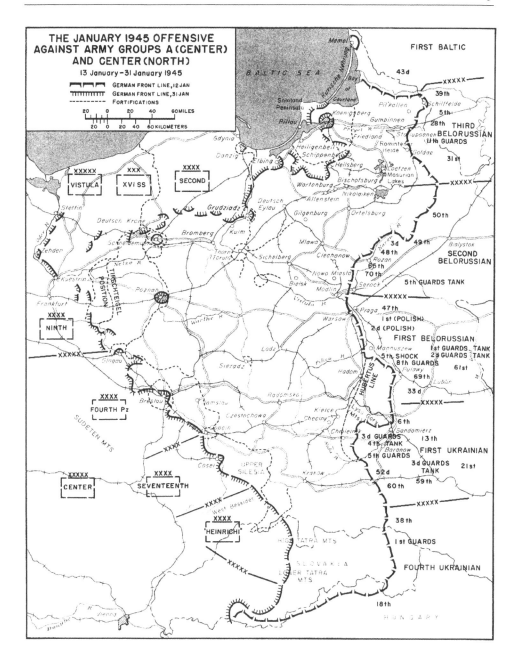

THE JANUARY 1945 OFFENSIVE
AGAINST ARMY GROUPS A (CENTER)
AND CENTER (NORTH)
13 January – 31 January 1945

GERMAN FRONT LINE, 12 JAN
GERMAN FRONT LINE, 31 JAN
FORTIFICATIONS

20   0   20   40   60 MILES
20   0   20   40   60 KILOMETERS

night, it gave an uncomfortable feeling since the enemy would be invisible until he was right before the trench.[6] The men did not like to go into the trenches and felt insecure. The *Volksgrenadier-Infanterie Regiment* 1098 took us over. It was warm, sunny weather.

21 JANUARY

Regiment 1098 took us over. About 35 soldiers were distributed among our men. This was supposed to be an entire battalion. The soldiers seemed very much the worse for wear. For days they had received nothing to eat, probably also a result of the fact that their trains elements were too far to the rear. My own experience is that it is every bit as important for soldiers to be provided with food as with ammunition. They feel that they have been abandoned in the trenches if they receive nothing to eat and to smoke. What I have heard many officers say, that the combat situation made it impossible to bring food forward, counts for nothing. In every case the ammunition made it to the front. To our left was an Insterburg *Volkssturm* battalion and, on our right, an Angerburg *Volkssturm* battalion. As our battalion command post we had a well-constructed and camouflaged bunker. The *Wehrmacht* battalion commander, who still commanded the 35 soldiers, was also stationed there. The bunker was about 50 meters behind the combat trenches. There was little room for two command posts. In addition, our surgeon also had to work there, since there was no other bunker available for him. The day remained quiet.

22 JANUARY

There were supposed to be artillery, anti-tank guns and mortars behind us. People even spoke of *Nebelwerfer* (rocket launchers). It was all a swindle. I believe that the responsible positions, all the way up to the very top, were in complete denial, deceiving their own selves. It was a very beautiful, sunny day and, in the morning, I walked along the entire stretch of trenches to the right. Everything was quiet there with no sign of the enemy. In the trenches there were only sentries at their

---

6   Translator's note – The field fortifications in question were constructed in haste, at the very last minute, by civilian work forces raised by the *Gauleiter* and, for the most part, were not laid out by military engineers, nor was their construction supervised by military engineers. This is only one example of the multitude of deficiencies, defects and errors in their construction.

weapons. The other men rested. They needed that rest. The previous nights had given little opportunity for sleep. Heavy firing, however, was audible from the left wing. There had been enemy contact there ever since 1000 hours. The Insterburg battalion had, in part, bolted, and the Russians had already pursued them into the rear area. The *Wehrmacht* cleaned up the penetration. The soldiers[7] had, in general, behaved well.

At 1200 hours I went over to the left sector of our trenches. A portion of the 2nd *Kompanie* was there. The entire 1st and 4th *Kompanien* were distributed in strong-points. All of our weapons were distributed in the trenches and abundant ammunition had been brought up. Some of the men had already been provided with German carbines. The 1st *Kompanie* had already had contact with the enemy and dead Russians had already been identified in front of the position. The company commander, Kopkow, was not to be seen in the trench. I positioned the men properly with their weapons, encouraged them and emphasized that they should only fire when they saw something, and then to take good aim. I also took part in the firefight with my automatic rifle and fired 60 rounds. There must have been quite a lot of dead Russians in front of our position. You could see them lying there. I remained in this sector of the trench until 1700 hours. During this entire time Kopkow was not to be seen in the trench, As I departed he finally appeared. *Gruppenführer* [squad leader] Köske had brought in a Russian prisoner. The prisoner stated that five infantry battalions were facing us and that the attack would come late in the evening or in the early morning hours.

I went back to the battalion command post. Scarcely had I arrived there when our battalion commander, along with the *Wehrmacht* battalion commander, hobbled into the bunker. Both had wanted to go to the left sector and both had been wounded by fragments. Klein had a fragment in his right heel. After he had been bandaged he said to me: "Just, now you must see that you are the only one capable of action. Herewith I turn the battalion over to you." Then we talked together for a long time. He spoke of how well we had understood each other and that he had full confidence in me. He thanked me with moving words for the good cooperation and for the help I had given him at all times. Then he had to wait for his transport to the rear. Wurach then entered the bunker and spoke with me at length. He said that he had confidence in the men of our battalion and that

---

7   Translator's note-In general, when the author speaks of "soldiers", he refers to the *Wehrmacht*, the regular army.

we would do our duty well. Klein told him that he wanted *Hauptmann* Batt to succeed hem. Wurach was to bring that into effect immediately.

From that point on I did not leave the bunker. There was great activity. Reports from the companies arrived constantly, and I sent messengers to them. Ammunition was requested. Here a weapon fell out of action and had to be replaced. Then the *Waffenmeister*, the armourer, was called for because another weapon had jammed. Rations had to be brought up. The wounded had to be removed. The *Wehrmacht* messengers came and went. The radio operator received reports from the regiment and passed them on. Wounded were brought in and had to be bandaged. Many of them had horrible wounds and wailed and groaned. I had to maintain my concentration so as not to lose perspective. Dr. Torkler also bandaged the wounded soldiers, for the *Wehrmacht* did not concern itself with its wounded. The vehicles were constantly underway. The wagon-drivers did well, for every time they had to drive through a stretch of woods to get to our bunker, and that sector of woods had already been under Russian mortar fire for a long time. It was amazing that there were no losses there. They had much work with the horses, especially in the pitch-black night. When the shells burst and sprayed fire and dirt they still made it through. Fortunately they also brought up rations for the men.

In the meantime, dark night had fallen. Firing from both sides constantly mounted. The Russians pounded our entire sector and the rear area with concentric artillery and mortar fire. At times the fire mounted to an inferno. Where were our heavy weapons that we had been told about? Nothing was there. There were ever more dead and wounded.

At about 1700 hours the *Wehrmacht* pulled its soldiers out of our trenches. Our neighbour on the left, the Insterburg battalion, bolted and the soldiers had to seal it off there, because now there was a gap and the Russians had enveloped our left flank. The Russians observed that the soldiers had been pulled out and immediately launched an attack on our 3rd *Kompanie*. The attack was repulsed. For a change, an officer again came from *VolksgrenadierInfanterie Regiment* 1099 and declared that we were attached to 1099. Even as we were discussing that, an officer came from *VolksgrenadierInfanterie Regiment* 1098 and said that we were still attached to 1098. Thus, right into the potatoes, then *Raus*, out of the potatoes. They no longer knew what they wanted. In any case, there was nothing to be heard from our side about artillery joining in the battle. The Russians could do whatever they wanted with us. We no longer had any fliers at all. Our own battery had gone into another sector. But they had only 60 rounds of ammunition and finally had to blow up their guns and abandon them. That had probably already come to pass, that the heavy weapons had generally been abandoned everywhere because, first, there was no ammunition available and, secondly, that there were no horses or prime movers to bring them out.

At 2200 hours a man reported to me who had escorted the wounded to the rear. He had met ten men from the 3rd *Kompanie* there. Inquiry at the 3rd revealed that no men were missing. But two hours later someone reported to me that the 3rd *Kompanie* had bolted. I immediately summoned the company commander, Rohse, and he told me that his company was, in fact, already short of men. He spread out the remaining men to avoid leaving gaps. Unfortunately, the trenches were then very thinly manned, because many men had already dropped out due to death or wounds. The company commanders of the 2nd and 4th *Kompanien* spoke with me. I asked them about the morale of the men. They told me that everything was still in order with them. I told them that they must take care, no matter what happened, that the Russians would be wiped out in an attack that was to be expected toward morning. They believed that they could assure me of that. At 2400 hours *Infanterie Regiment* 1098 moved its command post farther to the rear, and, after that point I no longer had any contact with the regiment. We had been left in the lurch. We repeatedly attempted to establish radio contact, but it was all in vain. And that happened just as things were getting hot in our position and it could become critical at any moment. We were left in the lurch. What were they thinking of?

23 JANUARY

Just past midnight men reported themselves sick from the trenches who had, apparently, lost their nerve. Dr. Torkler resolutely sent them back into the trenches. However, I had the impression that many failed to go back. It was hardly surprising that the old men lost their nerve, for they, too, noticed that we had no support at all from heavy weapons, whereas the Russians were free to pound us with their mortars unhindered. Hell was generally let loose out there. The Russians considered it important to soften us up so that their attack would run into little opposition, and also fired with their heavy weapons into the rear area to interfere with supplies. The shells fell so thickly that it was no longer possible to count them. The situation continued to worsen in the night and in the woods. At times we had so many wounded that we had to use several vehicles in order to remove them. Our losses continued to mount.

In the meantime the wounded *Wehrmacht* battalion commander had also turned over the remnants of his battalion to a *Leutnant*, who was by no means up to dealing with the situation. He repeatedly stressed that he and his few remaining people could not hold the blocking position. I later ran into him, all alone, without any men. Whether they were, by then, all wounded or dead I do not know. In any case, I learned from him that there was no longer any contact between the 1st and 2nd platoons of the 1st *Kompanie*. Apparently, there, too, the men had already bolted or been captured. Later I was never able to find out from Kopkow what had happened there. The 2nd *Kompanie* sent reports to me at 0300 hours that the men had become restless and would no longer hold. The gunfire got more and more intense. More and more of our weapons dropped out because their crews were either dead or wounded, but the men that were still in the trenches were brave and defended themselves to the extreme, they fought to the last.

I repeatedly got the impression that we had been left to our own devices, that we had been betrayed and abandoned. That impression was also strengthened because nobody was concerned for the wounded soldiers. Not even one medic had been assigned to us. The poor chaps would all have died if we had not cared for them. Thus the night passed for me with a great deal of work, cares and excitement.

On the outside, fate had once more decided against us. The Russians had, apparently, broken through everywhere, for, at about 1700 hours, a *Landser* leaped into the bunker and shouted, "The Ivans are coming!" I immediately ordered all of the men that were present at that point in the bunker to prepare to counterattack. They consisted of Dr. Torkler, medics Segatz, Gürtler, Ryba, Struwe, Steiner, Stachel, Aschmonat and a solder who grabbed a *Panzerfaust*. Stachel led us to a favourable position at a railroad embankment. We went into position there and soon heard the Russians approaching. They had already crossed our trench. I had everyone open fire with whatever he had. The *Landser* alongside us fired the *Panzerfaust* once. Apparently he tried to fire another round but never got it off. Unfortunately, either our machine gun failed to function or Aschmotat was too excited. He ran back quickly to fetch another, and also failed to get that to function.

We lay like that for about an hour facing the Russians. Finally they must have realized what a little bunch we were, and that must have irritated them. I noticed that several Russians leaped over the trench, apparently in order to bypass us. Then the comrades reported to me that they were out of ammunition, and I, too, had only a few rounds left. Now it was time for us to get out of there, for we could not allow it to turn into hand-to-hand combat against such overwhelmingly superior forces. I gave the order to retreat. Initially we ran back to the bunker, but it was already full of Russians. We went farther through the midst of the woods. *En route* we ran into yet another *Leutnant* with a few *Landser*, and proceeded, together, back to the forester's house. Fortunately all of my men made it back safely. In any case, I had the happy feeling that I had done my duty there and had made it possible by my conduct for many comrades, who were already retreating from the position, to make it back safely.

In the forester's house I immediately reported by telephone to *Volksgrenadier Infantry Regiment 1098*. More and more men kept turning up there, including Rohse, Stachel and Schimmelpfennig. Then a *Leutnant* came from *Regiment 1098* and told me that they had already heard at the command post that I had ordered the battalion to retreat. I was to be brought up before a court martial. I refuted this accusation as slander. Then a wild officer drove up with a *Sturmgeschütz* and ordered Schimmelpfennig to seek out men and attempt to regain the old position. What a venture! The people had no idea what had already happened and had even less of a hint of the overall situation. How could they, when I had been entirely out of contact with them for 24 hours? Now they were looking for a scapegoat whom they could blame for the situation and happened upon a little *Volkssturm* commander. In actual fact it had been insanity from the very start to commit us in that impossible forest position without any support from heavy weapons.

In addition, we had been told, when we were being introduced to the position, that the *Wehrmacht* would fall back from a more forward position to that position. However, all of us observed that they had already fallen back farther to the rear and only left 35 *Landser* in the trench with us. We had done nothing wrong. Naturally, it was also impossible for us to get back to the edge of the woods, since our people came under fire and had to fall back. Unfortunately, in so doing, Stachel failed to return. I later heard that he was wounded and captured. The Russians came over the open field toward us in great masses. The *Sturmgeschütz* only fired a few times into them and the Russians lay dead.

The forester's house came under mortar fire and we assembled in the woods. Infantry counterattacked forward, but we were not committed.

Suddenly an automobile drove toward it and I was horrified to see that *Hauptmann* Jamm got out of the car. Jamm came instead of Batt. He assumed command of the battalion and led it back to Tannenschlucht. We were again committed at a railroad embankment, for the Russians were advancing from all sides. We were still able to hold them off until darkness fell. Then the ammunition ran out and we were able to disengage. It would have been an easy task to halt the Russians with a few tanks or artillery. But it was not there. A few *Sturmgeschütze* were far distant. They fired a few rounds and vanished. Then there was nothing at all near us. Could we do anything more? We were all embittered that we were so impotent. And what had everyone told us? We had marching orders to Jänichen, to Wagner's headquarters. I had a group of 70 men with me. Jamm took off with the automobile. Most of our beautiful weapons remained in the trenches. The men had only brought a few light machine guns with them.

24 JANUARY

We marched all night. We bypassed Insterburg, which was already ablaze from end to end. Behind us the front was quiet again. The last wounded had all fallen into Russian hands. This time our losses in dead, wounded and missing amounted to about 300 men. We had again been properly shattered. Was the great sacrifice necessary? Above everything, couldn't we have been better committed somewhere with support from heavy weapons? There, from the very beginning, we had been committed to a lost cause.

The 4th *Kompanie* simply marched away with its company commander without waiting for orders. I next ran into it in Königsberg. There was already great excitement in Jänischen. Everything was prepared to move out. There I gave an extensive report to higher Party leaders over the entire series of events in the Eichwald position. This report was supposed to be presented to Wagner. I was released with the assurance that I had performed my duty. Then events moved forward, for the new marching orders read to Königsberg, and, indeed, on foot.

25 JANUARY

We spent the night in a farmstead by the side of the road. Several hens were quickly killed and they smelled delicious while roasting. We could not stay long anywhere, for the Russians were hot on our heels and no longer seemed to halt. We could only reach the individual localities on side roads, because the main roads were all occupied by the Russians or were under fire from their artillery. *En route* we saw the miseries of the refugees with our own eyes. Simply everyone was on the move. Each one had his bundle under his arm and marched on the road. We met long treks with farm wagons. In their midst, again and again, were *Wehrmacht* columns that ruthlessly cleared their way on the road. So many farm wagons, fully loaded with luggage and household goods, their families sitting on top of them, simply rolled into the roadside ditches and had to be left there. The slick, icy surface of the roads contributed to this. Everyone was in terror of falling into the hands of the Russians. Everywhere on the roads was a wild flight.

25 JANUARY[8]

We got as far as Friedland on byways. There I again ran into Jamm. There we were to remain and be committed in the Deime position. Since, however, we were without weapons or ammunition, and the men were tired and battered, rest came first. Then we were to keep on going, onward to Königsberg.

26 JANUARY

We came to Preußisch-Eylau. All of the roads there and in the villages that we passed were overfilled with refugee's wagons. We got the impression that all of East Prussia was on the move. But what did these people hope for? There was no longer any way to get from East Prussia to the *Reich*, for the Russians had cut off all of East Prussia. If they could only get across the Haff[9] they could still escape the Russians. Otherwise they would fall into their hands. Most of the refugees were ignorant of that. For most of them there was no more running away. Everywhere there were capsized wagons, household goods scattered on the ground. On the wagons small children cried, for it was cold and they had nothing to warm them. Cattle ran free in the fields, sheep and horses ran around. Most of the refugees had brought poultry with them. All of the farmsteads were abandoned, and whoever came upon them rooted around in the abandoned rooms and furniture. There was a fearsome mess in all of the buildings, as if the Russians had already been there. What would be the fate of all these refugees? One heard of the atrocities that the Russians perpetrated everywhere. Women and girls were indiscriminately raped by them. That was why all of these people were so anxious to escape the Russians, but they would not escape them.

---

8   Translator's note – The repeated date is as in the original diary.

9   Translator's note – The Frisches Haff, the sound between the mainland and the Frische Nehrung, the long sand spit stretching from Pillau the rejoin the mainland north of Elbing, east of Danzig.

In Preußisch-Eylau I was able to get warm underclothes and felt boots from the *Volkssturm Stabsführer*. I also supplemented my clothing somewhat, for part of my luggage remained in the Eichwalder Forest, the rest was with the trains elements that had become separated from us and attempted to make it through on their own. That was certainly anything but easy on these over-filled roads. We had already marched 130 kilometers and now I took the train to Königsberg.

27 JANUARY

In Königsberg the latest news was that my wife was in Königsberg and had already been looking for me. Our meeting place in Königsberg was the Postal Giro[10] Office. Here I ran into a great many of our people. Unfortunately, Dr. Torkler was not there. He was supposed to be in Jänischen. There was dreadful confusion in Königsberg, at the Party offices and in general. The Russians were also just before Königsberg. I was here for the first time since the last bombing attack of the previous year. I must say that I was overwhelmed by the impression it presented to me. The entire central city was totally destroyed. And had that, indeed, been the result of a single bombing attack? There was not one house, anywhere, that had not been damaged. Plain and simply, everything had been destroyed. Only ruins were left standing, and people lived in them. There must have been well over 100,000 people in the city. The suburbs were in better shape. There the fire and bombs had not destroyed so much.

I looked for my wife in Ponarth. Our joy was great that we saw each other again so unexpectedly. She had been unable to get out of East Prussia any more by rail, and finally ended up in Königsberg. At 2200 hours we were alerted that Russian armour was supposed to be in the city. Shortly thereafter we were able to go to sleep. It was a false alarm.

28 JANUARY

We received fur waistcoats and other warm clothing, a well as rations. We could take what we wanted, for there was no longer any organization. The Party *Führer* was said to have bolted. The battalion was divided into two companies and was

---

10 Translator's note – Referring to a specific system for transfer of funds by "girocheque" between one bank account and another, once operated by the post office in Europe.

170 men strong. The 1st *Kompanie* was under Szurowski, with what was left of the battery. The 2nd *Kompanie* was under Rohse.

29 JANUARY

There was not much sleep that night, for at 0200 hours we were ordered to move out to Ponarth, in the new position south of Königsberg. The command post was to be in the Schönbusch brewery. A second position was to be built there. The first position was held by the *Wehrmacht*. I had caught a cold on the march by foot to Königsberg and had to report sick. I went into my wife's quarters and laid down on the bed. Now we had to contemplate that some of the Russian positions were only three kilometers distant. My wife's dwelling was just behind the fighting-trenches. The Russians constantly shelled the entire sector and the shells impacted among the houses, nearly all of which were inhabited. Civilians were killed and wounded every day.

31 JANUARY

We were attached to Combat Sector Wachholz. Dr. Sauga, a capable man, joined us as battalion surgeon.

3 FEBRUARY

We moved our quarters to the center of the sector and were close to Ponarth, near the Fichteplatz. Now a time of martyrdom began for the men of our battalion. For the time being we were still able to entrench and fortify during the day. It rained and snowed frequently. Our men's things were no longer dry. Our sector of the trenches was quite large, so that the men were constantly in the trenches and had to fortify and keep watch. They had little rest and could not put their things in order. We received replacements. They were men from Königsberg. Some of them were no use to us and had to be sent back. A supply point, run by Sauvant, was set up in the Postal Giro Office. *Waffenmeister* Pötzing was quartered there and was responsible for supplies and provision of weapons and ammunition. He was quite effective. All of the weapons that we received were first inspected and sighted in by him. Every man could be confident in the certainty that every weapon that he received was in perfect order. Our vehicles, too, were well cared for there.

20 FEBRUARY

Now we received good equipment and clothing. Every man now had all that he needed. Above all, each man had a German carbine. The Russian rifles had been turned in. Firing practice took place several times in the week. We now had new and modern MG 42 and 43 light machine guns, as well as gas masks and gas capes, ammunition pouches and even a muzzle-cap for every rifle. Everything that a modern soldier might need was provided. Indeed, we were now better equipped than the *Wehrmacht*, and they envied us. Our uniforms were gray or aviation-blue. Only footgear was and remained scarce, meaning that there were still sufficient stocks in the clothing depots, but that they were not issued. We asked ourselves whom they were being held for. Königsberg was encircled, and would we be able to free ourselves? They might as well have issued all that they had. As for rations, there was still horse-meat. Other than that, everything was still there. Königsberg was provisioned with rations for a six month siege. We were assigned *Feldpost* [field postal] number 36100 ABJ.

I could not get things right with Jamm. He was a young jackanapes and too little of a soldier. He started out like a school teacher, not like a soldier. He spent too little time in the trenches and often spent the entire day in the office. He over-burdened the clerk with every possible kind of useless paperwork. Also, he was not man enough to straighten out the leaders and men when they needed it. He sent others to do it for him. He was obsessed with details, concentrated too much on them and ignored the big picture. He kept seeking advice from the combat-sector [higher ups] when he, himself, should have been taking action.

The time in our present position was no time of rest and recovery. The Russians shelled the city with their artillery and the trenches were constantly under their fire. We again had dead and wounded. There were losses every day. The men could only work in the trenches at night, and they were on watch in the trenches during the day. The men had a lot to deal with. The trenches were full of water and the Russians fired unmercifully on anyone who exposed himself outside the trenches. Only when the weather was misty was there any let up. In the meantime the enemy had advanced closer to our position. In some places he was only 1,000 meters distant. His observation was good. We still had good artillery that could also do a good job on him. Above all, our *Nebelwerfer* gave him a hard time. There were also daily losses among the civilians in the city. As soon as darkness fells, his night-flying aircraft swarmed in the skies. They were slow flying aircraft that flew very high and simply dropped their heavy bombs indiscriminately. We called these aircraft the "night-owls". Incoming rounds burst near our command post, without, however, disturbing us. At night he sprayed the entire area with indiscriminate machine gun fire, and so many brave men from our ranks again had to put their faith in God.

There were infantry in front of us. We visited with them in friendly fashion and kept a good eye on each other. I often went to the position at night with Jamm. It was then always a beautiful experience for me to experience the war in its fearsomeness. During the day one saw nothing of the war. All that one saw was that shells exploded, throwing up earth and filth. Now and then someone was hit by a flying fragment or a rifle bullet and sunk to the ground. At night, however, one saw the tracers flying around and the explosions of the shells and bombs. The Russians liked to fire a lot to disturb us. In part they used our mortars and machine guns. They must have captured enough of them. We, too, always had abundant ammunition. Our battalion had been filled out to 400 men. We again had a 3rd *Kompanie* under its good company commander, Tolksdorf.

Once Wagner visited our command post. He clapped my shoulder approvingly as he received my report on our service in the Eichwald Forest.

Janke came to us from a work battalion. His company had been captured. He brought us good horses. Quittkat also finally made it to us with a portion of his trains elements. Kopkow was often drunk out of desperation. He had entirely given up and sought comfort in alcohol. One night, when his men had to carry him back, dead drunk, from the forward position he was arrested and sent to the penal company. He was also demoted. Exactly the same thing happened to Schibilla, who had always been his comrade. He went off to the *Wehrmacht*.

5 MARCH

We had to turn over all the men born in 1901 and younger to the *Wehrmacht*. Unfortunately that took 28 of our best men. I also lost my comrade Höfner, with whom I had shared my joys and sorrows from the very start, and who had been my bunkmate in all of our quarters.

12 MARCH

I received the *Verwundetenabzeichen* [wounded badge] for the wound I had received in October.

20 MARCH

The company commander of the 3rd *Kompanie*[11] was pursued from his former military duty station. He was demoted by Wachholz on the basis of a report from Jamm and transferred to another battalion. Jamm did him an injustice. He was our best company commander. Naujocks assumed command of the company. Losses due to death and wounds mounted daily. Again the battalion melted away. One after another of our comrades had to depart. If the losses kept up like that it could not be much longer before we would be totally wiped out. We could no longer count on replacements. Our losses always seemed to be the men that had to man our heavy weapons, and it often got to a point where there was no crew available for the heavy weapon until another could quickly be trained.

Our men did not have it easy. If only they could have been given a few days of rest, but there could be no thought of that. To the contrary. We were now alerted more frequently and the men had to stand, day and night, without relief, in snow and rain in trenches full of water and do their duty, brave and true. The East Prussian people could be proud of these men. We now had only older men. The youngest was now 44. Many were 50 years and older. None of us had received any news of our families since mid January, for the mail had not arrived since then. Of the Russians, who by know had occupied our entire beautiful homeland, we heard only about atrocities. The men were uneasy and concerned about the fate of their families. Had all of them been able to flee in time before the Bolsheviks? Every one of us officers were concerned about them and spoke to them of courage when we, ourselves, felt our own hearts breaking because of the catastrophe that had come upon us. In East Prussia only a small bunch fought at Königsberg, and another little bunch in Samland. Could we, alone, destroy the Bolsheviks? None of us could be blamed if we lost our courage. Even among us on the staff nerves were on edge, and I often had to intervene to avert explosions. The commander must keep his head no matter what happens. The conduct of the men regarding the enemy was truly worthy of admiration. Despite all the daily losses and their grave concerns they remained in the trenches and defied the Bolsheviks.

---

11 This is not the original commander of the 3rd *Kompanie, Oberleutnant* Rohse *Studienrat,* [secondary-school teacher with civil-service status] at the Kantschule, but the new commander of the new 3rd *Kompanie* since the battalion was replenished on 20 February 1945, whom the chronicler considered the best company commander. Since 28 January 1945, Rohse commanded the 2nd *Kompanie*, because, at that time, the battalion only consisted of two companies.

Metgethen was recaptured and the Party and *Wehrmacht* opened the place for inspection. It was ghastly. Everywhere lay women and children that had, first, been raped by the Russians and then brutally murdered in horrible ways. Nobody was left alive. Our men heard all of that and they suffered greatly. My wife and daughter had been evacuated to Pillau and then came back to Königsberg. Now they were daily exposed to the shelling and I was deeply concerned for their continued wellbeing. The *Führer* had spoken and had told us that all we had to do was hold on, that the turning point would come in the immediate future. How often had that already been said to us from all places and it failed to happen. We would happily endure all of the difficulties for a long time if only once something good would happen for us on the field of battle. It required great faith if one was still to think of victory.

28 MARCH

We were relieved. It was about time, or there would no longer have been many of us left. The companies were to be initially withdrawn and set in march for Königsberg. A police battalion relieved us. They did not bring along many weapons. The companies were quartered in cellars in Königsberg.

I celebrated my birthday with my comrades in Ponarth.

29 MARCH

The battalion staff proceeded to the Postal Giro Office.

A new order awaited us there. There was to be no rest for us. The battalion was to secure the *Seekanal*[12] *by Holstein. We were attached to the 548*th *Volksgrenadier Division.* I made quarters for the staff in the Margen forester's house. The entire terrain was wet and swampy and there were several bunkers available that were above ground. It turned out that they were unusable and had to be dismantled in order to be rebuilt in another location. Freshly cut wood had to be brought in and the roads were, in part, bottomless. In several places the men had to work up to their knees in water, and they had miserable footwear.

---

12 The *Seekanal* was the deepened channel for shipping extending from the channel through the Frische Nehrung at the port of Pillau through the Frisches Haff, a shallow sound, up through the mouth of the Pregel River to the city of Königsberg.

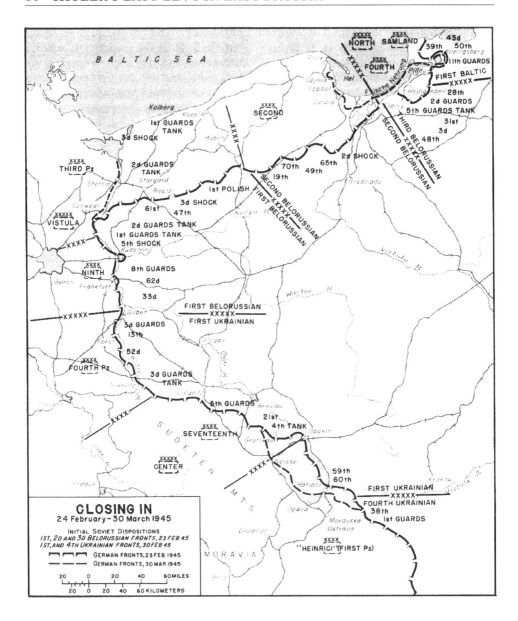

The 1st *Kompanie* had to do the worst work. In their quarters, too, they were miserably housed. One platoon occupied the first island and secured it against an enemy landing. The 2nd and 3rd *Komnpanien* were billeted in Nautzwinkel and were, at least, in houses, that had, of course, all been cleared of their residents. The 2nd *Kompanie* immediately occupied the second island of the *Seekanal* and also secured that against an enemy landing. The 3rd *Kompanie* built positions in Nautzwinkel. Therefore they had to start immediately with the fortification, there was no rest for us. The village of Nautzwinkel was still totally undamaged when we arrived there, although the Russians had already occupied the village somewhat earlier. The inhabitants had, for the most part, remained there, and now the women told us how the Russians had treated them. Without exception, every one of them had been repeatedly raped. Many had been carried off and nothing more was known of them. The inhabitants were very happy to again be freed by German troops.

It was very beautiful, warm weather and, for the time being, we were not disturbed by the Russians. Construction of positions went well. The men could even catch fish, thereby bringing a welcome change to our rations.

1 APRIL AND 2 APRIL

Easter. The first day of the celebration was quiet. I took advantage of the opportunity to visit the 1st *Kompanie*, which was farthest away. It rained, and the terrain in which this company found itself looked desolate. The poor men had already had to endure somewhat. They were relatively well housed on the island. At night they had to occupy the bunkers that they had built in the terrain, for all of the weapons were, naturally, installed and were constantly manned by sentinels. For the most part they secured toward the south. The *Wehrmacht* adjoined to our left, the 548th *VolksgrenadierDivision* to which we were attached. The men could have felt sorry for themselves, but they did their difficult duty undaunted. The company commander had arranged for a good noonday meal, and there was also a schnaps ration, so the man had something, at least, to more-or-less celebrate Easter. On the second day of the holiday it was back to work again everywhere.

2 APRIL

The Russians approached Königsberg closer from all sides and also shelled our location with their artillery. The quiet time was past. We were visited by aircraft day and night, and again they daily dropped their bombs on us and, by day, we came under heavy fire from the air. They strafed anything that they could see on the ground. We suffered our first losses. Every day was worse than the one before.

We were attached to the 561st *Volksgrenadier Division* and *Major* von Kleist was the sector commander. The Party also reported itself again and we now belonged to Combat Sector Liebe.

5 APRIL

The Russians daily raked us with their bombs and strafing. Our Dr. Sauga was seriously wounded while *en route* from the command post to a sickbay, as was one of his medics.

We had long since sought out the cellar of our forester's house, because there were no longer any windows in the living rooms, and it had also become too dangerous there. If, as experienced men of the *Volkssturm*, we no longer feared any danger, we still did not go out of our way to seek it out. The 3rd *Kompanie* alternated with the 2nd *Kompanie* on the island, while the 1st *Kompanie* remained on its own island. The company commander, Szurowski, had to remain on the island, himself. Platoon leader Krämer then led the rest of the 1st *Kompanie* to Holstein. The Russians had shot up several of the boats we used for crossing to the island, so that bringing the daily rations, which could only be brought over at night, was extremely difficult. The men on the second island lived by twos and threes in little huts which they had built for themselves from rushes and brush. At night it rained very often and the men were hardly ever dry. Therefore there could be no thought of sleep. In addition, the Russian aircraft closely observed the island so they could not stir by day. They could only move around at night. Fishing had long since stopped.

7 APRIL

At 0700 hours in the morning I drove to Königsberg to the Postal Giro Office. That day the Russians attacked Königsberg concentrically. The road through Metgethen was under fire. I still got through well. In Königsberg I met my wife, who now lived in Königsberg. The Russians had already captured several of the suburbs. I implored her to immediately leave Königsberg, which she promised to do. This time we parted with heavy hearts. Hopefully she would still be able to escape this time, in time. Again and again shells fell in the city from all sides. I left Königsberg, which made a desolate impression on me. On our return journey the road was under heavy artillery fire. Dead horses and men and smashed vehicles lay everywhere. Shells landed in front of me and behind me and destroyed the road. Nothing was to be seen of our own artillery. Several times I had to take to the ditches because of attack from ground-attack aircraft. Nevertheless, I made it safely through. Always the shells struck where I had just been, but none of them got me. The Russians pushed forward toward Königsberg from all sides. It was, otherwise, interesting to observe how the attack and the defense against it proceeded. Shells burst everywhere, and, every time, a fountain of earth rose high. Here an infantry company assembled and launched a counterattack, there a mortar section dug in. Artillery changed its position. I saw the division commander, himself, on the road, making his arrangements.

I made it safely to Nautzwinkel. Several houses were hit there this day and destroyed. Others burned

8 APRIL

Early today we heard two hours of steady drumfire on Königsberg. Then heavy bombers flew incessantly over the city and dropped high-explosive and incendiary bombs. I was able to observe it very well from our position with the binoculars. The city was ablaze from end to end and I saw an immense amount of smoke. I was very concerned for my wife and daughter. Had they been able to get away yet? In the morning two men drove with a horse and wagon to Juditten to fetch ovens for the bunkers. They never returned. Probably they took a direct hit. Our efforts to find out what happened were fruitless. We were under heavy fire for the entire day, and again there were dead and wounded. And we had no doctor. It was extremely difficult to transport the wounded, since nobody could allow themselves to be seen on the road. Yet it had to be done. The wounded had to be transported to the *Wehrmacht* dressing stations. Again and again the drivers [horse-drawn] had to be called on, and, despite the heavy fire, they did their duty. In the kind of total war that was now being conducted, everyone was being called upon equally and even the drivers of the trains-element's wagons were exposed to exactly the same danger as all of the other comrades at the front. I could rely on the drivers, who were always right on the spot when they were needed. They had left Nautzwinkel a few days before in order to protect the horses and wagons from bombs and shells. Therefore, when they were called, they had to drive the dangerous road twice. I can only praise the drivers highly.

During this night several thousand inhabitants were evacuated from Königsberg. Hopefully my wife and daughter were among them. 30,000 civilians were still said to be in Königsberg.

We were all under fire, for there was no longer any rest. We had not slept for days. We carried an armchair into the cellar, and at night we sat there, and anyone who had some time, sat in it and tried to sleep. At least he closed his eyes and attempted to sleep. In the dark Gürtler drove to Königsberg with four vehicles to get rations. He made it back alone with one vehicle. The others were missing. Certainly those brave men had also fallen. Unfortunately we saw no more of our Quittkat.

9 APRIL

As on the previous day, the village and the entire rear area was under heavy fire. Ever more of the houses around us in Nautzwinkel sank into ruins. Portions of the village were plowed up by bombs and shells. The 3rd *Kompanie's* quarters burned down. The abundant ammunition could not be saved, and exploded with a loud blast. Nobody was injured. Then our 3rd *Kompanie* command post was hit by a bomb and several men were wounded. The 1st *Kompanie* had to pull back individual sentries from Holstein forest, for the Russians were advancing closer to Nautzwinkel. Quite heavy bombs hit near our command post. The house shook and heaved, but was not damaged. If the Russian fliers aimed when they dropped their bombs we would have had more losses. This was better for us than aimed bombing would have been. Stables and barns on our farmstead had already been hit repeatedly. Our house stood up above its surroundings and, curiously, had not been hit. We could only use the road by running and leaping from cover to cover. Everywhere the fragments flew about our ears.

Otherwise the Russians employed a slow-flying airplane at night that dropped quite heavy bombs. As soon as darkness fell and the daytime fliers vanished, these night-fliers appeared and circled overhead incessantly until morning. We called them the "night owls". It was an uncomfortable feeling to hear these aircraft circling high above us in the night. They dropped their bombs indiscriminately and nobody and nothing was safe from them. During the day you could observe the airplanes carefully and see whether you would be fired upon. The Russian airplanes could only aim by aiming the entire airplane.

10 APRIL

We were attached to the 5th *Panzer Division*, which had rolled up in the night and was to launch a counterattack. After good initial progress the attack ground to a halt. We were in the trenches in the highest level of alert, for the Russians had, at the same time, concentrated forces for a major operation. In the morning we worried about who would land the first blow. Our 5th *Panzer Division* was quicker. Unfortunately they had lost many heavy weapons in earlier fighting and the Russians had superior forces. Heavy artillery had gone into position near us, but the ammunition was lacking. And what could one division do against several armies equipped with the best of heavy weapons? The Russian infantry no longer held their positions when they were attacked, but they almost always enjoyed superior numbers.

The propaganda from the Committee *"Freies Deutschland"*[Free Germany] gave us a lot of trouble. Especially in the evening loudspeakers were set up across from us and, in the name of this committee we were called upon to throw down our weapons and change sides. Unfortunately, very unfortunately, several divisions of German soldiers fought against us under the command of *General* Seydlitz and others. Thereby brothers often faced each other in battle. In our sector there were no line-crossers, but we often heard that entire companies had changed sides as a group.

The superiority of the enemy forces facing us was always too great and we lacked heavy weapons and air support. We were only a little bunch left that fought there and defended East Prussia, which had been entirely cut off. A second little bunch still fought in Samland. What did all that amount to against our eastern enemy who attacked with overwhelmingly superior forces of men and matériel? The heavy battery beside our command post could only fire one round every half hour. We in East Prussia had certainly long since been written off by the army supreme command. If they were still constantly telling us that we should hold on, that events would turn in our favour in the immediate future, considering the circumstances, one would have to have great faith. We hoped and we waited from one day to the next as if for a miracle. It would not be our fault. We had already held on for quite a while. Jamm and I constantly encouraged the men and put fresh heart into them, for there were, naturally, some among us who were anxious. Many times I, too, had minor doubts and asked myself whether this still made any sense and whether the sacrifices that we also had to make daily were not in vain.

One of the 1st *Kompanie* billets took a direct hit that buried ten men. There were four dead and six seriously or lightly wounded. So it went, on and on. The battalion again melted away. Every single man that fell was a shame. There was no communication with family members, for there was no longer any mail. We were completely cut off. We heard very little from the world.

11 APRIL

The *Panzer* division was gone again, and we were left to our own devices. The infantry adjoining us sent a *Panzer* forward every now and then that only fired a few rounds. Ammunition wa s in short supply everywhere. There was heavy fighting for Königsberg. We learned that *General* Lasch, the defender of the fortress, had not had the barricades that were built there manned, and would surrender Königsberg because there were too many civilians in the city.

Again we suffered heavily under bombs and artillery fire. We had no news from the 1st *Kompanie* on the island. On this side the Russians had already advanced past it. We observed the island through a scissors-telescope and could see that the reeds on the island were burning. Otherwise there was nothing to see. We had orders that the island was not to be evacuated under any circumstances. It must be held.

We learned from the remnants of the 1st *Kompanie* that were in the bunker that a bunker held by five men had been taken by the Russians. The men were captured. As evening approached another bunker with four men was captured by the Russians.

12 APRIL

The 28th *Jäger Division* was now there and it was rumoured that they were to relieve us. There were a large number of stragglers in their ranks. They wanted our weapons, which, however, we would not give up.

At 2200 hours Jamm suddenly lurched into the command post and declared that our dock, from which our companies were transported over to the island, was in Russian hands. We had to launch an immediate counterattack. The battalion staff (15 men) prepared. On our way we ran into 15 *Landser*. I took charge of one half, Jamm the other. We slowly and cautiously approached the dock. Then we determined that it was a false alarm. There were no Russians to be seen. Our position ran 100 meters distant from the dock.

The battle was raging in full force, and, for me, the battle at night presented a beautiful picture. Very lights rose high from both sides and lit the landscape light as day. Right afterwards, it was all the darker. Tracer rounds whizzed back and forth. Artillery and mortar shells could be seen bursting on both sides. At times there would be bursts of wild machine gun fire. The Russians also used our machine guns. It was easy to distinguish them from the Russian machine guns because they had a far higher rate of fire. I could watch for hours. Unfortunately, however, it was war, and bitterly serious. If not every bullet found a target, still, many of our comrades were hit and sank to the grass, dead, or had to be carried off, wounded. The battle demanded victims, again and again, from among our men. Hopefully it was not all in vain. I positioned 12 of our messengers to reinforce our position alongside our 3rd *Kompanie* and went back with Jamm and Struwe.

At 2400 hours Jamm brought news that we would be relieved during this night. Two navy motorboats were available to carry our two companies over. I immediately went through the night back to the dock with Struwe and could again observe the wonderful display of the battle. Shells bursting near us and fragments and machine gun bursts humming past did not disturb us. We had long since become accustomed to such fireworks. I arranged for the transport of both companies back from the island. It would have to go quickly. It would all have to be done by daybreak. The relief must be completed and the battalion departed from Nautzwinkel. The crossing went very quickly, for everyone was concerned to get away from there as quickly as possible. The 1st *Kompanie* got away from the island without the Russians noticing anything. They did not do anything to disturb us. The men were all very happy. The warm rations that were brought up were well received. The 3rd *Kompanie* covered the crossing of the two companies from its fighting trenches and was only able to disengage from the enemy, itself, when the *Landser* of the 28th *Jäger Division* occupied the trenches. As day started to dawn, all of the 3rd *Kompanie* with its entire trains elements pulled out of Nautzwinkel. Nothing was left behind. All of the weapons and the abundant supply of ammunition were brought along. Several machine guns and 2 cm automatic weapons, however, had long since been put out of action by enemy fire. We happily left them behind.

I, myself, could only follow a few hours later with the staff, as I had to properly turn the command post over to the *Jäger*. How beautiful Nautzwinkel had looked when we first occupied it. Today there was hardly a house left that was not damaged. Our house, however, was still undamaged. The war had treated this beautiful village harshly. During the night the dead were hastily interred. The relief took place without losses and unnoticed by the Russians. The Russian fliers still pursued us on our march to Kaporn with their strafing. All three companies bivouacked in the woods. The sun shone and it was already warm. It seemed like a holiday to us. It was so beautiful and peaceful after all the difficult days and weeks. The men lay down on the grass and slept. I still had things to do and could not rest. The rest did not last long, for the Russian fliers also found us there and, flying low, strafed us. At 1700 hours we got word to proceed to Fischhausen. We got into makeshift quarters there in the middle of the night. Everyone, however, was happy that they had gotten out of the hell of Nautzwinkel. Our battalion still had 120 men. The sacrifice demanded of our battalion had, therefore, again been very great. It would have been well worth it if it had brought us victory. So far, I had experienced great good fortune in coming safely through this mess. It was only because not every bullet finds a target. Otherwise there would no longer have been anyone left on either side. We did, however, lose a lot of vehicles, and the loads now had to be distributed among the other vehicles, which meant that, on occasion, the wagons had to be overloaded. It made for miserable going if we had to move off of the paved roads. Nevertheless, we were able to bring everything along. The company commanders were strictly instructed that, at all costs, they must bring along the weapons and ammunition.

13 APRIL

We were to proceed to Neukuhren. First, however, all the men were mustered once more. *"Tauglich* [able bodied] *1"* were to remain with the *Volkssturm. "Tauglich 2"* were to go to the work battalion, and *"tauglich 3"* were to be released. Then it was changed so that *"tauglich 1"* and *"tauglich 2"* were to stay with the *Volkssturm.* Jamm proceeded to Neukuhren with a 20-man advance party to set up quarters there. Liebe came to me and was astounded that we had been relieved. "Now you can rest up in Neukuhren. It is still quiet there", he said. How unsuspecting and uninformed the officers were. They never knew what the Russians planned and had in store. I then learned that Jamm had arranged for the relief on his own initiative. In fact, he had, himself, written out a slip stating that, by order of the *Reichsverteidigungskommisar* [*Reichs* Defense Commissioner] for East Prussia, our battalion was to be relieved from the Nautzwinkel position. By chance I happened to get a look at this slip. He went to the commander of the 28th *Jäger Division* with this note and the relief then took place. There had been no such order from the *Reichsverteidigungskommissar.* Jamm then got written certification that the relief by the 28th *Jäger Division* had properly ensued.

At about 2200 hours we finally got the promised lorries and off we went. *En route* I received orders that the battalion was not to go to Neukuhren, but to Palmnicken, for the Russians were already advancing on Neukuhren. And it had only been a few hours earlier that Liebe had told me that the Russians would do nothing with Neukuhren. I was to be assigned quarters in Palmnicken by the *Ortsgruppenleiter*.[13] Unfortunately, everything was already full of refugees and we camped, again, in the woods. It had been a long time since we had gotten any sleep.

The Ortsgruppenleiter was, otherwise, quite brusque and rude, so I had to reprimand him. Similarly, I had a disagreeable clash with a fat high Party leader [*Parteiführer*] in Fischhausen. What reason did these men have to treat me rudely? Everywhere we had to stick out our necks for them so that they could stay at home and keep up their life of gluttony. However, there was not one single Party leader enrolled in our battalion. Apparently all of them had more important work to do, even though now all of East Prussia had been occupied by the Russians and there was nothing left for them to do. One time we had *Kreisredner*[14] Weise with us for eight days, during which he proved himself to be quite nasty fellow and, from the moment of his arrival, devoted his efforts to getting away from us. That caused us no grief, and we were always happy if we were not burdened by the leaders.

That, at least, was the case until Jamm came to us. He always endeavoured to be in the good graces of the party. In that respect I had been on a better basis of understanding with our previous battalion commander, Klein, who, like me, did not care for them at all. Perhaps the success of the Russians had something to do with the fact that, in contrast to us, the Red party leaders were constantly with their people in the trenches and ruthlessly drove them forward. With us, these lordly people were too precious for service in the trenches, where their spotless uniforms would, doubtless, have been soiled.

Unfortunately, our 1st *Kompanie* had not received the rerouting order. It had departed earlier and ended up in Neukuhren.

14 APRIL

Throughout the day we bivouacked in the woods. I busied myself with rations, and the kitchens were able to provide us with a hot meal. At 1700 hours Jamm arrived and reported that the Russians had penetrated to Neukuhren in the morning and they all had to flee precipitately. The staff messenger also arrived. We have heard no more of the entire 1st *Kompanie*, nor of the messengers of the other companies. Probably they had all been captured. Unfortunately I had

---

13 Translator's note – The *Ortsgruppenleiter* was the Nazi Party Local Group Leader.
14 Translator's note – The *Kreisredner* was an official "speechmaker" for the *Kreis*.

already sent my baggage along to Neukuhren, so I again lost all my worldly goods. All day long motorized and horse-drawn vehicles of the *Wehrmacht* passed through Palmnicken. The hospital was evacuated. I was invited to supper with relatives of our chauffeur and was supposed to sleep there. Unfortunately, once again, things turned out otherwise.

At 2300 hours word came that the Russians were right before Palmnicken. Therefore I had to turn out and set the companies and trains elements in march, initially to Littausdorf. I was barely in my quarters when word came that the companies could not move forward with their vehicles on the jammed roads. Therefore, up again and working out remedies. Then things got moving. At 0400 hour I set out with Gürtler. Jamm wanted to follow with his automobile. In Littausdorf we were to be shown into the position. When I arrived there hell had already broken loose. The Russian fliers were already in the air and raked the *Wehrmacht* column and ours with bombs and strafing. All of the farmsteads around were already ablaze. Palmnicken, which we had just left, burned fiercely. The field-airdrome in Littausdorf was filled with German aircraft and was under Russian artillery fire. They did not hit any aircraft, but no aircraft took off. They had no fuel. Certainly, the Russians captured all of the aircraft intact. Bombs and shells tore into the tightly packed driving columns and tore apart men and horses.

The whole picture gave the impression of flight. Everywhere lay dead solders and horses and smashed vehicles. Wounded horses had to be shot and pushed to the side to clear room for the moving columns. Several of our horses were also wounded and the vehicles had to be left behind, because the others were already overloaded. The kitchens, too, could no longer move forward and were lost to us. Private automobiles, filled with soldiers, were simply hurled into the air by the air pressure of the exploding shells and smashed. Jamm, too, had to get out of the automobile with his chauffeur and seek cover, whereby the driver was mortally wounded. He and the automobile had to be left behind and could not be salvaged. All of the residents of the surrounding villages were on the road, fleeing before the Russians. The Russians mercilessly shelled these columns, too, and dead and wounded refugee-women and children and dead horses alongside their shot-up vehicles presented a ghastly scene everywhere. Horses that had been shot wandered around and the refugees watched in horror as the farmsteads they had just left went up in flames. Where were they to flee? There was no longer any way out for them from this horrible confusion. If they were spared by the shells and bombs, then there was Russian captivity, and they knew exactly what that meant for the women-nothing but rape and violation. Many simply left their vehicles behind and attempted to escape to the safety of the Pillau harbour. There was no longer any way for them to get away with their vehicles. The roads were fully jammed with *Wehrmacht* vehicles.

If it would only get dark soon, so that the Russian fliers could no longer see. But the sun shone and glaringly illuminated the whole fearful misery. For the soldiers it was a terrible feeling to have to watch, helpless against the might of the Russians. Were we truly at the end of our strength? In the *Reich* the Russians stood just before Berlin. From the west, the British and Americans approached Hannover, Thüringen and Bavaria. What would happen? We received the *Führer's* order for us to read: "Every soldier that falls, wounded, into enemy hands is a traitor and his family must pay the price." Again and again we heard that the *Landser* were desperate and no longer held their positions. Some left their weapons and ran to the rear, but many others ran over to the Russians. What good were their weapons? They could not attack airplanes and armour with their rifles. There were no longer any heavy weapons to be seen with us. There were no longer any tanks at all. In addition, the Russians constantly dropped leaflets saying that all who surrendered now could expect good treatment from them. The Committee *"Freies Deutschland"* recruited for Russia and sent German soldiers under German officers against our lines. A fearful suspicion crept over us, but we still strove against the thought that this would be the end. However, what we experienced and saw daily and hourly truly seemed to be the end. But even in this difficult time and need we never saw even one Party leader among us.

Our companies were well dispersed and suffered no losses. I was constantly concerned with the trains elements, such as were still with us, that they came along with us. Especially since, on our staff wagons were all the vital papers from the orderly room with the list of names of the entire battalion and of the wounded and fallen. Under no circumstances could these papers be lost. We also had rations with us. Liebe appeared at 1200 hours and ordered that we march to Pillau. There we were, ostensibly, to be transported across to the Nehrung. Under constant fire we marched along the Samland coast to Tenkitten. There I met with Jamm, who provided coffee beans and we brewed some good coffee for us. I received special orders and had to remain in Tenkitten. This day the battalion was to march on to Neuhäuser.

In Tenkitten was a large clothing depot, and I attempted to get underwear there to replenish my kit. Initially I was refused everything. The depot was supposed to be cleared out by lorries. How that was supposed to happen remained a riddle to me, for a big barn was filled with shoes, boots, clothing and underwear. No matter how many lorries tried, this supply dump could no longer be carried away, for the Russians were already shelling Tenkitten and, at any moment, the barn could go up in flames. Someone should finally be sensible and issue these stores to the passing *Landser*. So often have I seen giant rations and clothing dumps that could not be touched right up to the last moment, and then had to be burned or fall intact into Russian hands. How well could the *Landser* have been clothed and the victuals given out to the remaining civilian population or issued to the passing elements of troops. But the responsible *Wehrmacht* officials learned nothing to the last. After much back and forth I finally received what I wanted. That night I even got a few hours of sleep.

16 APRIL

Early in the morning the Russians also shelled Tenkitten. They thrust forward with all their forces to bring things to an end. We were ever more compressed. Many comrades allowed their courage to sink and no longer believed that we would ever get out of this witch's cauldron. There was only one road still open. I explained to them that I was firmly convinced that I would make it out of this last mess. Everywhere, so far, we had just managed to escape from the Russians. The clothing depot was plundered by the passing *Landser*, refugees and foreigners. The mountains of underclothes and clothing were trampled under foot and everyone sought out whatever fitted him.

Then I received orders to immediately proceed to Neuhäuser, and we made our tortuous way through the exploding bombs and shells past the *Wehrmacht* columns to Neuhäuser. From there we went right on to Pillau. In the woods before Pillau there was rest. The weather was beautiful. I rode with Struwe on bicycles to the city and we also met Heiner and Weise from Goldap at the *Leitstelle*.[15] The battalion followed on to the city. In Pillau, too, shells burst. Already hundreds of thousands of East Prussian refugees had been shipped from Pillau to the Reich or to Denmark. Seldom had a ship been loaded without Russian interference. Ships had also been hit, and, every time, there were more or less wounded and dead among the refugees. The steamer *"Gustloff"* was said to have gone down with 4,000 refugees.[16]

---

15 Translator's note – Information center to help troop locate their units.
16 Translator's note – The actual death toll when the *Gustloff* sank was 5,348.

Our new orders read, "Cross to Neutief and bivouac on the Nehrung at kilometer-stone 18.8. The battalion had a strength of only 70 men. That night, unfortunately, the trains elements was not transported over, and we would see them no more. We camped on the Nehrung in the woods in small foxholes, by twos and threes. That night we could sleep in peace. It was the first quiet night in long, long weeks. And the peace there was downright heavenly. We had had no real rest since 17 January. The Russian fliers could no longer discover us in the bunkers and the night passed without interruption.

17 APRIL

The sun was already warm and we relished the rest with all our senses. Everyone could do what he wanted and passed the time however he chose. Again they were all happy that they had again escaped the Russians intact. We heard that the *Führer* had said that we would only have to hold on for a short time. Berlin would never be Russian and Vienna would soon be German again. We no longer knew what to think. Who or what would now save us? I no longer saw any way out. I worried about my family. Hopefully they had gotten out of Königsberg in time.

I spent much time standing on the beach and watched how the ships sailed to Pillau to bring out *Wehrmacht* and refugees. Russian fliers would score a direct hit on a ship and it would sink immediately.

18 APRIL

This day, too, remained quiet for us. Jamm came at 1600 hours from a discussion and declared that the East Prussian *Volkssturm* was to be disbanded. There were only 1,200 men remaining of the original 130,000 *Volkssturm* men. We had lost nearly 100 %. Truly a great sacrifice, and what had this great sacrifice been for? There could no longer be any belief in a good end to this war. Would this sacrifice, too, have been in vain, exactly as after the First World War? It would be fearful and sad for our fatherland.

200 volunteers were to remain to protect the *Gauleiter*, the others were to be shipped back to the *Reich*. Nobody voluntarily stayed behind as guard for Koch. We were ready to continue to do our duty as *Vollkssturm* with weapon in hand, but not to protect the *Gauleiter*. Then, according to a new order, the leaders and Party members were to remain. One found none of these, either. Again we slept this night in peace and quiet. The trains elements had not yet been brought over.

19 APRIL

We were to march to kilometer-stone 21.5. It had now, finally, been decided that we would be shipped back to the *Reich*. We packed our knapsacks and moved out. It was hard for us to leave this beautiful little place where we had enjoyed the first rest after difficult days. At kilometer stone 21.5 we surrendered what weapons we still had and marched to the resting place. It was a field-airfield with earth bunkers. There we spent the night. Our victuals were nearly gone, for it had been a long time since any had been issued. It had been a long time since we had all been truly satisfied.

20 APRIL

We came to Kahlberg in beautiful, warm weather. I arranged for rations, which were given to us in abundance by the *Wehrmacht* and, for the first time in days, we could again eat until we were full. There were quarters, too, although everything was overcrowded, and we were able to wash and shave and again look like proper soldiers. Jamm brought out his coffee beans again and we made ourselves quite comfortable. I nearly forgot the most important thing. Along with other comrades I was awarded the Iron Cross 2nd Class. It was awarded by the general of the 4th *Armee* for the fighting at Insterburg in January. It had, indeed, been a long time since then, but we were all happy. I proposed to Jamm that we rest here for another day to wait for our trains elements. However, he did not permit discussion of it.

In the course of our march along the Nehrung from Pillau, we ran into the last refugees from Königsberg and the vicinity. They all had to march on foot to Kahlberg, which was 60 kilometers from Königsberg. Several were picked up by passing *Wehrmacht* lorries. Otherwise they had to march on foot. One has to imagine that in order to be clear what was expected of the refugees, for the most part women and children and old men. The only piece of good fortune was that we had beautiful, warm weather. But not all of these people were in condition for a march. At first, all of them still had much baggage with them, but then they were no longer able to drag it along and simply had to leave it along the way. During our march we saw articles of luggage lying everywhere. When these poor refugees, who had now lost all their worldly goods, arrived at their new destination, they would have no more than what they carried on their bodies. Would they then be given clothing? Most of the women had set out on their flight in their light street shoes, and those were already worn out. Many had lost their heels. They spent the night in the woods, on bare ground.

They were also given nothing to eat *en route*. Those who failed to bring anything with them could scarcely make it to the end of the flight due to hunger. It was even worse for the people that had small children. I believe, for a fact, that many small children died *en route*. So much is said about women and children during the First World War and also in this war that were carried off on foot from Russia and Poland to distant parts of the world. When one saw this misery, then one had to make involuntary comparisons and it could not have been any worse then. However, they bore their difficult lot with patience. All hoped for a better future and they would not remain behind for the Russians under any circumstances. Who knew what the future would bring? These refugees truly deserved good treatment in the future and every concern for their well-being. It was very fortunate that we on the Nehrung were no longer harassed by Russian fliers.

21 APRIL

We marched to Stutthof. There were no rations. Billets were awful, in a machine hall whose roof had been shot to pieces. It rained and, for days, refugees had lain in this room, hundreds of men, women and children intermingled, jammed together awaiting their ship. There were no latrines for the many hundreds of people, and the place was befouled and stank horribly. Neither were their any facilities for washing.

We also had to spend the night there because it rained. Otherwise we would have preferred camping in the woods. Word was that men born in 1900 and 1901 were to be drafted into the *Wehrmacht*. It sounded like a joke. Those already serving at that time in the *Wehrmacht* had not yet even been issued weapons. How would they arm the new soldiers? Already there were not even enough rifles at the front for the infantrymen. It felt good, however, that we were no longer troubled by Russian fliers on our entire march.

We got to Nickelswalde, after marching 160 kilometers. From there we were to be transported to Hela by ship. There we learned that the men born in 1901 were immediately to report to the *Wehrmacht*. Unfortunately our paymaster, Gürtler, left us. We all deeply regretted his departure, for he had been with us from the beginning.

Once more I attempted to persuade Jamm to wait there for the trains elements. He was not to be convinced. Our trains elements were finally lost, with all the rations and all of the important papers that we had saved to date, and with all of the men's baggage. We would not be able to notify any relatives of the resting places of their fallen men, for all of the files of the orderly room were also on the trains-vehicles.

We concerned ourselves with tickets for the ships, and loading was to take place at night. Thus it was that we were to finally leave our East Prussian homeland. We all took it very hard, because we had little hope of ever seeing our homeland again. Behind us there still remained a little band of *Wehrmacht* men that were to hold back the Russians. They would not succeed, for the Russians could no longer be held. And we had all left everything behind that was dear and sacred to us. Our homeland had been destroyed, the families scattered to the winds. Our men had heard nothing from them for months, and our lives were also disrupted. We had lost everything and were poor as mice. And what would the future bring?

It lay dark before us. Certainly we had nothing good to expect from the Russians.

23 APRIL

At 0200 in the night, along with many refugees and wounded, we were transported to Hela and loaded there into the 4,000 ton ship *Weserberg*. It was to go to Denmark. The weather was superb and that was good, for the ship was overloaded and the refugees camped on the upper deck with all that they had saved. During the night, however, it was uncomfortably cold. One time there was cold food, otherwise no warm soup or cold coffee. The hygienic facilities were awful. With this degree of overloading they could not serve even a fraction of the passengers. I sought out the ammunition magazine and lived there with other comrades among the depth bombs and artillery rounds.

25 APRIL

The passage went smoothly without problems, no airplanes and no enemy ships crossed our course. Throughout the day I stayed at the railing and watched with interest everything that took place during the journey on our ship and on the sea. As a result of the miserable quarters we all had lice. The ship was terribly filthy. The people sat around impassively, and did not even complain that no-one gave them anything to eat. They were probably sufficiently happy that they had escaped the Russians. All other misfortunes they could bear. They talked about what they had lost and with what might lie ahead. They all suspected that they could expect nothing good. All had one thought, when and how would they all meet up with their family members? They had all suffered a great loss, and asked, again and again, why fate had hit them so hard.

In the morning we arrived at Copenhagen, in Denmark, and were directed to the Citadel. We had hoped that we would, at least, be able to rest a day there. None of that. We were given only two hours time to see the city. We exchanged our money for kroner and went out into the city. It was marvelous to stroll around there. There was no trace of the war. All of the shops were open and anything could be purchased there. What a difference there was between here in Copenhagen and what we had left behind in East Prussia. In East Prussia there was destruction everywhere. For long months we had moved among destroyed houses that had been abandoned by their occupants. There was only deprivation. Here everything was available. The people were clean and well dressed, though all the women seemed to go in for a lot of makeup, for they all had their faces painted. First I bought myself some chocolate. Unfortunately, it only looked like chocolate, it was *Ersatz*. The sausages were strongly colored and inedible. Thus here, too, there was much that only appeared to be good.

26 APRIL

We arrived at Frederizia and spent the night there. In the morning I strolled through the city and dined fabulously at noon. I got two large pieces of roast pork. It had been a long time since I had eaten anything other than horsemeat. I was able to eat until I was full.

28 APRIL

We arrived in Flensburg, thus, back in Germany again, where we were to be discharged. Nobody at the *Leitstelle* knew what was to be done with us and they initially sent us to quarters. Flensburg, too, was untouched by the war, and the deepest peace ruled there. We were very conspicuous with our uniforms, for all the soldiers here went around spick and span. It was obvious that the front was far away, while our uniforms were very worn.

Indeed, we came from the front.

29 APRIL

Early in the morning we went for delousing, and then it was rest. Food was practically unavailable for the men. I was very well housed and was happy about it.

1 MAY

The *Führer* took a coward's way out and evaded responsibility by taking poison. He is dead, and many of his Party leaders committed suicide. That is the end.

We were to go to Rendsburg for discharge.

2 MAY

We finally got there in the early morning and our train was shoved onto a siding. It was said that the Tommies (English soldiers) would be there in an hour and that all the soldiers would become prisoners of war. With Jamm and several other men we decided not to surrender as prisoners and drove back to Flensburg.

3 MAY

In Flensburg we were discharged. The war was over for us.

Epilogue
9 May

In closing I will only say that my time of service in the East Prussian *Volkssturm* was a beautiful time for me. Our battalion was one of the few that was constantly in action, and I am proud of that. We did our duty just as did every soldier of our incomparable *Wehrmacht*. When times are quieter, people will also remember the *Volkssturm*, and this diary will contribute to the fact that the East Prussian *Volkssturm* will not be forgotten. The sacrifices that our battalion, too, made, were immense, and the fallen and wounded comrades deserve to be remembered. Twice our battalion was reconstituted, and, as the last survivors of the East Prussian *Volkssturm*. We had only 70 men left.

It must be remembered that our men were all over 45 years old, and many older than that. One must especially acknowledge what the men in the trenches accomplished. We were in the fighting trenches without a break from 17 January to the end of April, and fought, shoulder to shoulder, with the brave soldiers of the *Wehrmacht*. Often, however, we were left on our own, and performed exactly the same sort of heroic deeds. Only one who was actually at the front can properly appreciate what our men accomplished and what all of us truly experienced. Despite the deep concern that every one of us had, for we had all lost our homeland early in October 1944, and our families were in flight or had already gone missing, every man did his duty to the utmost without grumbling.

None of us knew what would become of us after the unconditional surrender of 8 May, but we knew it would be nothing good. However, as I knew our men, they would all take up the struggle for existence under the difficult conditions and put together a new life. I, myself, also had the feeling and the rock – solid faith that I, too, would find employment under the totally changed conditions. In these conditions one could only look to the future. Everything that lay behind us was past.

Bruno Just
Hameln, 11 June, 1952
Sertürnerstraße. 38a

Former address in the homeland: <u>Goldap Ostpreußen – Schuhstraße. 4</u>

Lightning Source UK Ltd.
Milton Keynes UK
UKOW06f0254180116

266538UK00004B/50/P